# TEXTILE VOICES — MILL LIF[illegible] Y

PUBLISHED BY BRADFORD LIBRARIES & INFORMATION SERVICE
BRADFORD HERITAGE RECORDING UNIT
EDITED BY OLIVE HOWARTH

PHOTOGRAPHS AND ORAL HISTORY

First published by Bradford Libraries and Information Service.

British Library Cataloguing in Publication Data
Textile voices: mill life this century.
1. West Yorkshire (Metropolitan County). Bradford. Textile industries. Personnel. Social life, history
I. Howarth, Olive II. Bradford Libraries and Information Service
942.8'171

ISBN 0-907734-19-7

This book is subject to the standard conditions of the Net Book Agreement.

Printed by Thornton and Pearson (Printers) Ltd.

Edited by Olive Howarth.
Project Co-ordination and Picture Research by Tim Smith.
Editorial Assistance by Carol Greenwood.
Transcription Supervision by Janet Godbold.

*Cover:* J. Whittingham and Sons, Wool Merchants, Canal Road, circa 1900.

*Title Page:* Weaving shed, Wetherdair Ltd., Church Street, Manningham, 1940.

# CONTENTS

*Burling and Mending of cloth, J. L. Booth, 1949*

# ACKNOWLEDGEMENTS

Over the past six years B.H.R.U. has carried out an extensive interviewing programme in the Bradford Metropolitan District. This collection includes over two hundred life story interviews with members of the textile community. This is the most extensive oral history project ever carried out on a single industry in this country, and forms the raw material from which the following extracts were selected. The accompanying photographs have been gleaned from a complementary archive of thousands of pictures, originally taken for family albums, or by press and commercial photographers.

Such a massive undertaking makes it impossible to thank everybody who has contributed. Over the years B.H.R.U. has been reliant not only on the unfailing support of Bradford people, but also those of its many past staff who have been so committed to its aims. However some individuals and organisations merit particular thanks: Carol Greenwood and other members of the Central Library for help, advice and enabling the production of this book; the Secretarial Services of the Central Library for typing support; Janet Godbold, David James, Harry Watson, and Laurie and Laureena Broom for their helpful suggestions; Graham Hall and Woods Visual Communications for permission to reproduce photographs; and Rob Perks for the introduction.

We trust that most of our interviewees will have the opportunity to read this book, together with many others who shared similar experiences. Hopefully all its readers will gain new insights into the working lives of people who helped to make Bradford the wool textiles capital of the world.

*Tim Smith, Project Co-ordinator.*

*Looking across the Thornton Road area of central Bradford towards Manningham Lane, 1926*

# INTRODUCTION

'A Surprising Place' was how Bradford cheekily promoted itself in the early 1980s. And it worked: in a simple phrase the national preconception of Bradford as a sooty Yorkshire city of dark satanic mills was turned on its head. The coach tours flocked in. Suddenly tourism seemed to provide at least part of the solution to a steady decline in the city's staple industry: textiles. But then, in a sense, Bradford has always been a surprising place.

Even in the late eighteenth century, when mills were springing up all over northern England, Bradford lagged behind other West Riding textile towns like Huddersfield and Halfax. Largely this was due to the opposition of local people who understandably cherished the 'verdant fields and fruitful gardens and purling trout streams' of their sleepy market town. But, once the first mill opened in 1799 and the transition from domestic hand production to mechanised factory production culminated in the arrival of power looms at the beginning of the nineteenth century, Bradford never looked back.

In the space of fifty years Bradford was transformed into the worsted capital of the world with a population of over 100,000, 129 mills and one-third of the total labour force of the UK worsted trade. New-found wealth on an epic scale constructed Bradford's biggest, most opulent industrial and civic architecture, some of it inspired by the Italian Renaissance and dealing in such world-beating superlatives as 'longest mill frontage' and 'greatest number of looms'. Huge mills and larger-than-life owners like Illingworth, Lister and Foster predominated. The opening of Titus Salt's Saltaire Mills in 1853, where raw wool entered and finished cloth left, symbolised the industry's audacity. Yet it was a success grounded not only in cloth production but in merchanting, centering on the grandiose Wool Exchange and the warehouse quarter known as 'Little Germany', and in dyeing. Ripley's dyeworks in the Bowling district was the biggest in Europe.

The other side of the coin was not so happy: housing and sanitary conditions were appalling. The average age expectancy in 1840 was eighteen years, with half of all children never reaching their fifth birthday. Yet people continued to flock to Bradford for work from the surrounding countryside and from further afield. By 1851 10% of the town's population were Irish-born, establishing the close link that was always to exist between textiles and imported labour in Bradford as successive ethnic groups have been recruited: first the Irish, then the East Europeans, Europeans, West Indians and Asians.

By the turn of the century much had been done to improve Bradford's environment. The number of mills had grown to 350 but 'Worstedopolis', as the city was popularly nicknamed, remained under increasing pressure from changes in fashion, foreign competition, and a number of countries which had erected tariff barriers against Bradford products. However, five-sixths of all wool consumed in the UK still passed through Bradford at some stage of its production or marketing. Bradford's unique Conditioning House scientifically tested wool and cloth from all over the world. Wool merchants still thronged the cafes clustered around the Wool Exchange discussing world prices and sealing multi-million pound deals by word alone. Yet more ominiously Bradford was providing spun yarn and combed wool to its developing foreign competitors. Integrated 'sheep to suit' mills like Salts teetered on bankruptcy as the industry moved to specialisation and smaller units. Both world wars boosted trade but the story of Bradford textiles this century has been one of decline.

By 1983, when the Bradford Heritage Recording Unit set out to tape-record the memories and experiences of Bradford's textile workers, we were faced with a depressing picture of an industry at its lowest ebb. In the preceding twenty years over sixty per cent of its workforce had been shed, a loss of 45,000 jobs. The skyline, once punctuated by hundreds of competing chimneys, had become a silent landscape of empty and derelict mills. Yet as we watched (and photographed) the physical destruction we talked to those who remembered what Bradford had been: who had in one lifetime witnessed its fall from world dominance. We recorded life-story interviews with nearly 200 textile workers over three years: the oldest born in 1889, the youngest in 1959. At the outset we were determined that every sector and job in the industry would be covered: from the President of the Confederation of British Wool Textiles through owners, merchants, overlookers, dyeworkers, trade union leaders and weavers, to doffers and bobbin-liggers. We wanted to know every facet of life in a community where virtually every family was connected in some way to textiles. We wanted to talk to men and women, black and white, young and old.

Oral history was an obvious way to do it. Not only because it captured the authentic voices and unique experiences of a disappearing lifestyle, but because it was the **only** way of discovering the impact of textiles on everyday life. The mill owned your house, it controlled your working day, it decided your friends (and your partner), it determined your health, it organised your leisure time, and in some cases told you what to think, where to worship and how to vote. What written accounts existed tended to be from the the point of view of those great employers: somewhere along the line 'ordinary' people's stories had been lost. So much of what we recorded on tape had never been written down. Sometimes, as with sexual harassment, victimisation and racism, this was because that sort of thing never **is** written down. Sometimes because feelings and relationships are intangibles and **can** only be spoken. Sometimes because it had never seemed important before. Bradford was, and still is, so steeped in the culture of wool that to ask people questions about it seemed too obvious. But ask we did and some of the answers were surprising, as this book shows.

But oral history was also a way of rescuing the individual from the crowd, and from the stereotype. Suddenly personality, character, warmth and humour sharply replaced the amorphous mass of 'textile workers' and 'migrant workers'. Glib historical generalisations peddled by countless historians fell away to reveal a rich variety of experience. When we listened to people we were listening not so much for facts, names and dates, as for attitudes, feelings, emotions and beliefs. Teasing out the feelings of a twelve-year old half-timer on their first day beginning a 36-hour week on mornings alone with school in the afternoon required sensitivity and patience. Especially as the person was likely to be casting their minds back some seventy years. Interviews ranged in length from one hour to seven. The approach throughout was a flexible and open-ended one. We rejected a rigid questionnaire in favour of a chronological framework of themes based on a full life-story in which interviewees could speak candidly with the minimum of direction. Working life was placed within the broader context of background, neighbourhood, childhood, education, family life and leisure time. A team of interviewers were carefully chosen and matched to each person: and the same ethnic origin where this was possible. Each interview was tape-recorded, copied, documented, summarised and in many cases transcribed, then assessed in the light of the overall project. Gaps in coverage of particular processes, mills or age groups were plugged as time went on: unusual and surprising stories checked with other interviewees. The industry itself and the trade unions were very supportive, as was the local press and radio who ran regular appeals and news items on the project's progress.

What emerged was that, in truth, until the Second World War many working class children in Bradford had little choice: they were destined to enter the mill like their parents and grandparents before them. It was difficult to escape the shadow of the mill and childhood would be spent on errands to the mill. School was a waiting room: scholarships were rare for boys, unheard of for girls. The wage was simply too precious to give up. The job when it came required no interview, no application form and only the most cursory medical inspection: a word by a relative in the right ear was usually enough. Once initiated (often quite brutally in the case of boys) the novice entered a highly disciplined, hierarchical and sex-segregated world. Yet it was also a close-knit world of mutual support. Dips in trade which brought short-time working and lay-offs were weathered through a mixture of neighbourly generosity, inventiveness, pawnbrokers and allotments. A sense of determination, pride and humour permeates stories of the most astonishing hardship.

The majority of spinners and weavers were women, their overlookers men. Sexual harassment and abuse of authority through preferment of favourites were not uncommon. The reality of working conditions rarely accorded with factory inspectors' reports, and occupational hazards were legion: not just accidents when limbs were lost but deafness, and anthrax from woolsorting. Canteens and welfare provision came very late, in many cases not until the 1940s and 1950s, and even in the 1930s stories were rife of pregnant women working right up to delivery. Textile trade unionism was notoriously weak, hampered by a history of consistently low wages, labour shortages, importation of cheap labour, a diffuse workforce and, most recently, computerisation.

The Second World War marked a turning point for the industry. With an immediate post-war slump textiles seemed to offer fewer prospects than the emerging national health service and new firms like Baird's televisions, International Harvester's tractors and Grattan's mail-order. Re-equipping with faster looms from abroad and the introduction of a continental shift system came too late to prevent a strong downturn. Protection from foreign competition through the Multi Fibre Agreement undoubtedly helped and the industry looked abroad to recruit a labour force it could afford: first East European Volunteer Workers, then Italian women, finally Asian men. But bankruptcy, diversification and belated investment in new technology in the 1970s slashed the labour force and created record unemployment. Textile engineering, particularly loom making, also suffered: one of the oldest firms, Hattersley's of Keighley, closed as the interviewing programme began. Textiles was no longer Bradford's largest employer.

This book is not a comprehensive and definitive history of Bradford's textile industry: it is an impression of an entire culture and way of life which extended beyond the workplace. The individual voices are allowed to speak for themselves: it is their narrative. If what we are told is at times surprising then this oral history will have achieved its purpose and emphasised the importance of listening to the past more carefully.

*Rob Perks. Curator of Oral History at the British Library National Sound Archive (former B.H.R.U. Co-ordinator)*

*Names such as Silk Street and Patent Street served to remind the Lister's workforce that their houses belonged to the company, whose Manningham mills dominated the skyline.*

# HOME AND NEIGHBOURHOOD

"We lived in a house that belonged to Thomas Burnley's"

"People round here were brought up on textiles you know, they lit their fires with mill bobbins."

*M. Born 1934*

"There were a lot of mills around where I lived. At twenty five past seven the siren would go to say to folks you've got five minutes, and then the streets would be awash with people."

*F. Born 1938*

"We lived in a house that belonged to Thomas Burnley's, they owned our houses, if you could call them houses. My father worked in woolcombing, at Regina, up Leeds Road for most of his life. He worked on nights for about 18 years, so we didn't see all that much of him, because as he came in we were ready for going to school, and he went immediately to bed. I remember my father never had a holiday. You only got a week off and didn't get paid for it. So my father used to go into work that week and he would be white-washing the walls or whatever and they would pay him a wage for doing that. He had an allotment, so we lived practically off the land apart from the meat, which was bought quite cheaply to suit the wages he was getting. There was always something on the hob, either some stew going or meat, and a lovely hot oven, that quite often you had to cool down sometimes. But coal was very cheap you see, it was reasonable for our pockets at that time.

Although I can remember 1932/33 we went through a very bad period when there was no work. There was one fire put on at the morning, long enough to cook a meal and then we all went to bed to keep warm. We used to take either a hot brick or an oven plate to keep warm and if there was any fire left in the grate it was carried upstairs on a shovel to warm the room up there so that it wasn't wasted. But we slept five children in one bed. There was another child in a cot, there was my parents' bed at the foot of our bed, in one bedroom. One bedroom only, one living room only, a very tiny cellar-head, one cold tap and the toilets were outside. They were the old types that were emptied every week. Now if you came in the house, the houses were scrupulously clean. There were stone floors and those floors used to be scrubbed every day! And we used to have some floor covering in the centre that nobody hardly walked on. They called it coconut-matting, but that would have been taken outside and beaten two or three times a week. The house itself had what is described today as a chaise longue, and it was horsechair, and no way did you want to sit on it. There were never enough chairs to go round, so if the oldest brother came in he just tapped you on the back, and you automatically stood up to let him sit down. It did go on seniority except for the tiny ones, and they got priority till they were old enough to find their place in the household. In her early married life my mother worked in the mill. She worked in what they called 'back-wash minding'. Then, when we were young, she used to make pies and pastries for local shops. She didn't bake them, she prepared them and then she would come home to see to us.

The neighbourhood had very cramped quarters and there were no secrets because you could hear everything through the walls. But there again you didn't sort of need that privacy because you were all the same. Your parents even played with you. We'd play rounders in the street and you would have to do the fielding for your parents. In summertime your parents would be outside talking till nearly ten o'clock at night, but all the work would have been done, everything would be settled."

*F. Born 1924*

"Sunday there was a dinner made, and that was it. It was Sunday School at morning, Sunday School in the afternoon, and at night we often used to go visit my Aunty and Uncle at Wood End. But Sunday was a different day, a day apart. You could go for a walk but you didn't play games, and you wasn't allowed to take a ball out. You'd one set of clothes you'd to put on on a Sunday and you took off Sunday night, and you didn't look at them no more until the next Sunday. It was the same with your fire-irons, you'd two sets, one brass and one steel. Your steel ones were out all week and at weekend your brass ones were taken out from under the bed. They'd these little bits

*Back to back housing, Harris Street, off the bottom of Leeds Road, 1950s.*

of distinction that they had for the weekend."

*M. Born 1917*

"My grandfather was a countryman. He cared for the horses, he kept dogs, not as pets but as working dogs to keep the rats down and to guard the place. He kept hens in any old corner he could find, and he always ran a cock with them so that he could incubate his own eggs if he wanted, and so he could cook a cock chicken for his Christmas dinner, because that was a luxury; you had it once a year. He had an allotment where Morrison's Victoria Supermarket is now, and he grew anything he could, tomatoes, cucumbers, vegetable marrows. He remained a countryman at heart all the time he was in Bradford."

*F. Born 1929*

*Knocking up in the morning, c.1910.*

"Pawnbrokers used to be very prevalent at that time, and every Monday she'd call in to my mother and she'd say, "I'm going to the opening-out, is there anything you want?". She'd say, "I'll look for you some bedding or something if you want it." Now the opening-out was people that had pawned something and failed to redeem it after a certain time, so then they sold it at a reduced price. They sold ladies' Monday, so she spent Monday afternoon going to the pawnshops to see what they had to sell. A lot of the neighbours used to visit the pawnbrokers.

They would take their husband's suits or the young men's suits, and on a Monday morning you could see them go in, and they'd go and redeem them at Friday so that they could have them for the week-end, and then back again they would go."

*F. Born 1904*

*Washday, 1940s.*

"A lamplighter was a full-time job and he used to supplement his wage by using the stick he turned the gas lamps off with on a morning, to knock people up for work. He used to tap on the bedroom window with the stick. When we went to live down South Parade you could hear these people going down to Raspin's, the combing shop on Valley Road, and they'd clogs on, and shawls, had the older ones."

*M. Born 1921*

"This is before the war like, when we had nowt. My granny only had ten shilling pension, so she used to go out about four o'clock at morning to knock all the tram drivers up. And then she used to come back about half-past-five, and then my mother used to get up. Well, we always had a bed downstairs because my grandma was a diabetic and she was always ill. And then when my mother used to get up at half-past-five I used to get up with her. And downstairs we had gaslight, but we couldn't afford pennies for the gas, so what my granny used to do, we either had a candle or we'd a paraffin lamp, and then I used to get in her bed till it was time for school. Then my mother went out knocking-up from say half-past-five up to about quarter-to-seven, then she'd have summat to eat, then go into the combing for seven o'clock in the morning. She used to come home for dinner, because it was just at the bottom of the street where we lived, she had three-quarters-of-an-hour for dinner. Then she'd go back and stay there while five. This is before the war like when they were on three days a week."

*F. Born 1927*

"Trade were very, very bad when I got married. At that particular time we worked Saturday mornings and I didn't go into work that Saturday morning. I was afraid of telling anybody I was getting married because they'd have thought "Well, she's in the family way I expect," which she wasn't. But you see I was only nineteen and I wasn't 'loosed'. So I got married at the Registrar's. And I hadn't the tram fare home, so William Henry Woodrow, who was my best man, who went to Sunday School same as what I did, paid the bus fare home. And Lily Horn what stood for Margaret, she bought a cake from John S. Driver's in Gaythorne Road, and the four of us sat down to a boiled egg and a piece of cake. Any rate when I went to my work at Monday, Pullet had me in the office. "Now then lad," he says, "they tell me you've gotten wed?" I said, "I am Mr Pullet." "Well," he says, "tha'll be wanting some more brass." And he gave me a shilling rise. One of the weavers found me a cottage at Wibsey, on Harbour Road, McGees Back Yard, and we bought a house full of furniture at two and six a week from Moulds in Manchester Road. And that's how we set up."

*M. Born 1909*

"We got married in 1948, and we lived in rooms for the first eight years because you had to have so many points and so many children before you could get a Council house, and no way did I want my family while I was living in an upstairs bedroom and an attic. So we started saving up to buy our own house, which took some doing because we were already having to pay for the living quarters we were in besides. The funny thing was that the house we bought belonged to Lister's originally, but they decided to sell them. It cost £600, £300 deposit and the rest on rental purchase. It took us nine years to buy that. But it was a lovely little house, side scullery, two bedrooms and an overall attic."

*F. Born 1924*

"I was going in the Wrens at seventeen-and-a-half and I wanted to see the world. I mean, all I'd seen was the back of Lister's Mill. Never had a holiday in my life. Couldn't afford, never been out of Bradford. Never been out of Manningham let alone out of Bradford. So at seventeen-and-a-half I was going to London by myself in the Forces, war on, of course, that great big world out there for me. I was going to be a film star, I was going to be all sorts like, in your little mind, anywhere but the back of Lister's Mill. But where am I now? At the back of Lister's Mill!"

*F. Born 1923*

*Haworth early this century, taken from outside the Liberal Club.*

# CHILDHOOD

"He used to make me little guns with the mill bobbins"

"I remember Billy being born. I remember him being born right well because my mother said, "Oh no, not another lad!" she cried! She said, "Oh not another!" And I had him till he was six years old. I had to take him with me everywhere I went because she had him like, as they said in them days, it were in the 'change'. Not planned, it wasn't really what you'd call wanted, but it happened and that were it. And I used to have to take him everywhere. But I'd take him because I could get in the pictures you see. She'd give me tuppence to take him to the pictures, and it were the only way I could get any money to get out was to take him with me. I'd take a little tin of Nestlé's Milk to dip his dummy in, and then I'd sit in the pictures. And I thought, "Well at least I've got a night out," otherwise I'd have been playing Tin Can Squat in the street with the rest of them."

*F. Born 1929*

"We were the average family, just keeping us head above water as you might say. But school was a problem. My mother was a Catholic, my father was a Protestant, and this is where the trouble came. When the 1914–1918 war started my father went into the army and my mother sent us to St Anne's School. When my father came on leave we'd to go back to Holy Croft School, and then when he went back we'd go back to St Anne's. That was the to and fro'ing of my schooldays. We'd used to play football at St Anne's, but I'd never any right boots. I'd a pair of old boots with some studs brayed in, and across the toe-cap at the front it was all split, and everytime I kicked the ball my toes came up through the cap, and then I'd to hobble about getting my toes back into the boot. And I remember we used to come from St Anne's playing taws, right from St Anne's Gate, on North Street, right the way through to Parker Street, playing marbles in the gutter. There was no traffic about at all. And in summer when the gas tar melted in the nicks of the sets, we used to collect tar balls. At weekends we'd break into Hattersley's yard, unofficially of course, round Parker Street this was. They made wood packing cases for the looms and they had stacks of timber, and we'd get a board about twenty foot long, put it on a slope and be sliding down it. I suppose the men were annoyed at Monday when they found the timber pulled about but we didn't break anything."

*M. Born 1909*

"My father was a woolcomber. He also worked as a backwash minder and various jobs in the combing. And during the Depression days he used to have to go looking for a night's work. Sometimes he'd walk as far as Charlestown Combing Company at Baildon from Manningham to look for a night's work. My mother used to say to me, "Now don't go away, because if your father gets a night's work you'll have to take him his supper down." It would usually be sandwiches tied up in a 'jock' hankie, a red and white spotted handkerchief. And so I used to have to wait, and if my father didn't come home for eight o'clock we'd know then that he'd got a night's work. And I used to have to go down wherever he'd told my mother he was going to seek a night's work, to take this supper down to him. Sometimes you were allowed in the building, they weren't quite as strict in those days with the security, so I used to go in sometimes. And he'd tell me to stand near the backwash, which was a container that used to wash the wool. It was the first stage of washing the wool and of course the heat was tremendous. He used to have me standing there for a few minutes and then he'd come back laughing at me. But there was no dole money and if my father couldn't find any work he used to have to go up to Drummond Road and chop firewood, or if it was winter he'd to go snow shovelling to earn a food ticket. And I always remember taking the food ticket down to John S. Driver's, and the treat was a ninepenny parcel, which consisted of a few potatoes and rabbit. That was a real luxury! But I remember once when he had no work coming home from school and we had no furniture, and later on I found out it was because we couldn't pay our rates and the bailiffs had come in and marked the furniture. My mother was in tears, I remember that very plainly."

*M. Born 1921*

"My dad had some allotments in Heaton Woods and he used to go up and bring back cabbage, rhubarb, and we'd have rhubarb and custard, and my mother would bake a few coconut buns. But mostly it were stews and cow-heel. I went miles doing errands for people, Oak Lane, Duckworth Lane, Toller Lane. And when you got back they'd give you a penny. You used to take it home and give it to your mother and she'd put it in an old handbag and keep it, because if the gas conked out she'd say, "Go and get that bag from under my mattress and bring fourpence down," and we knew we had gas for a couple of nights. But I remember once I went about ten errands for a penny. And sometimes if you took a penny home my mother would say "Get to Broadbent's and get an egg." You could buy an egg for a penny. You'd to bring it and boil it yourself. My mother would cut you a bit of flat cake, and then all your brothers and sisters would get to know so they'd all come in and have a dip. The yolk went with one dip of the flat cake and then they'd run out to play again. I used to think, "My God, that's charming. I've run all over for this."

*F. Born 1922*

"My mother got sixpence a week for knocking-up if she were lucky. Sometimes they'd wait till they owed her a pound then give her a club cheque instead and she'd get my Whitsuntide clothes with that at Parker's or Dixieland in Manchester Road. She were forced to buy me knickers and that for Whitsuntide because my great-granny used to lift your frock up to see if you'd new clothes underneath! We'd go all over showing us new clothes to relations and neighbours, and if it was only halfpenny they'd give you the halfpenny to make sure you got something. Instead of buying us toys at Christmas they used to buy us happen a liberty bodice and they'd get them miles too big. If you were four they'd get them for a six year old and put tucks in them so they'd last. Same with your flannelette skirts. They kept you well wrapped up, they wouldn't let you have a summer frock on till May went out. Because a lot of people before the war (WW2) suffered terrible before they could afford a doctor. If you'd what they called 'growing pains', they'd rub your legs with olive oil and say "It's only growing pains," you know, stuff like that."

*Carr Steps, Bankfoot, 1926.*

*F. Born 1927*

"Our elder brother was brilliant at school. He was top of his class and he was put forward for a scholarship. Out of his class there came a clergyman, a doctor and a solicitor

*Learning about shopping, 1925.*

and he was top of that class! But my parents were both afraid that they were tying themselves. He would have had to stay at school until he was sixteen and they would have to buy the uniform and they felt he would have been at a disadvantage if they couldn't afford it, and they didn't let him go. And they regretted all their life that he didn't go. And he ended up in the mill, and yet it was wasted talent."

*F. Born 1904*

"In the early days of the Depression (about 1927), when I was at Green Lane School, we used to get free dinners, free breakfasts. We used to have to go out to the front of the class for a ticket to show that you were entitled to a free meal because we had no money coming in, the family had no money. It was embarrassing, but with being young you just passed it off. Sometimes the other children used to plague you, you know, because the dress that we had

*Queue for potatoes in Bradford, c.1910.*

we used to get free from the Cinderella Club. The jersey was something like the Cub's uniform today with 'Cinderella' printed on the top of the sleeve."

*M. Born 1921*

"He used to come and watch us play football did this schoolteacher, and if I scored a goal he used to give me a penny. I know on one occasion I scored six goals against St Patrick's, and he gave me sixpence. Now that was a fortune! We had to provide us own shorts and black stockings and they provided a stocking top. My first football boots were ordinary boots, and my father put some strips of leather across instead of studs. I'd be about thirteen, going into the first team at Drummond Road, when my two sisters, who were working then, clubbed up to buy me these football boots for Christmas. I'll always remember that first pair. Then when I left school I played for Manningham Mills."

*M. Born 1921*

"We were coming home from school one day, taking a short cut, coming through Shipley Station and across Potter's Pits. And there was a big pipe across Bradford Beck, which was always referred to as Black Beck, although we could have called it any colour because when it was running off from the dyeworks it used to be red, green, all kinds of colours. And we used to walk across this pipe. Anyway, this day something had gone wrong with this chap's horse, and it had finished up in Black Beck. And as we were coming home they'd hoisted it out and were carving it up ready for carting off to the knacker's yard. We stood about and had a look as kids do, then we were glad to get away from it all at the finish. Between the canal and the Black Beck, opposite the bottom of Water Lane, was Wilson and Tattersall's Worsted Spinners. And in summer they'd have the door open and us lads, we'd lie at the other side in Water Lane heaving stones across and through the door, and they used to come out and threaten us, but they couldn't get at us because the canal hadn't been drained at that time."

*M. Born 1917*

"He'd a good sense of humour had my dad. At Christmas time if we had some oranges he'd juggle with an orange and throw it up in the air and put a fork in his mouth and catch it. He used to make me little guns out of mill bobbins from the spinning. He'd put a slot in the top of the bobbin and put an old clock spring in, and it would fire match-stalks."

*M. Born 1921*

*Half-timers outside Haggas's Mill, Ingrow, Keighley, 1908.*

# FIRST JOB

"The mill just seemed to swallow you"

"I was twelve when I went half time to Dawson's at Thornton. I laugh today when they're trying to get the 34 hour week; we did 36 hours on the morning turn! I passed twice for secondary school; then I couldn't go because I was working. I'll never forget the first Friday I came home with my wage. I sat down for tea and I got a kipper. I'd only ever had jam and bread before. Ooh I felt like a right man! It was only your father got kippers, things like that."

*M. Born 1906*

"I worked half-time. I went to school in the morning and into the mill in the afternoon, and I got two-and-nine pence one week and three-and-nine the following week. I went by myself to this mill. I knew they'd set me on. But you'd to go to the Town Hall, and if you hadn't so many attendances at school you couldn't go half-time. They gave me a note from school to say how many attendances I had, then I took it to the mill, and yes, I could start. Half-past-five, get up, make a fire, make a cup of tea, go to the mill for six o'clock and come home at quarter-past-eight for another cup of tea. Go back at half-past-eight and then come home at half-past-twelve for my dinner. It was my own idea but my parents didn't say, "No you don't," because they knew that little bit of money was coming in. I was tired and sick and fed up, but I knew once I'd started I'd have to keep on going. And I did that till I was thirteen and then I left school altogether and went to work full-time. And I got nine-and-six a week then. But the mill, when you're a little girl of 12, to get up at half-past-five every morning is a poor life for a girl."

*F. Born 1900*

"Lister's Mill must have took everybody from the back of that mill, Farfield Street, Chassum, Beamsley, Silk, Patent, all went down to Lister's Mill. I said to my mother, "When I leave school can I work in a shop?" She said "You're going in the mill where they've all gone."

*F. Born 1922*

"I mean there were four daughters and one son. Well the son had the best education because he was the boy. My parents were of the thoughts, "Well girls don't need educating, they're going to get married." And so we weren't educated, and that's something I've always regretted. So I went in the mill. I thought it was a very hard way to earn a living, and as soon as I could get out of it I did!"

*F. Born 1924*

"And so she took me that Monday afternoon at quarter-past-one, and I can remember going up in a hoist and a man pulling it with ropes, not like the hoists today you know, it were pulled by ropes, and handed me over to the overlooker. And when all the machines went on I just nearly ... I was petrified, absolutely petrified ... I mean a room with about fifty machines in, and they all went on! I felt I were going to collapse where I was. I were only thirteen of course. Anyway my father warned me, he said "Don't go for the glass hammer." So he warned me this you see, but instead I went for the leather oil can. And of course the overlooker he were annoyed, so he got the lads together, it were the boys that had sent me, and he got them together and give them all a job, and give them a bit of alley strap. It used to knock all the bits of wool, you know all the waste, it used to send it all under the frames, so when the walking boss came round it were all tidy you see. Oh it were a big alley strap, and it were all leather, and if they didn't behave themselves they got a bit of this alley strap. Anyway, for a few weeks we started at six o'clock in the morning. We had breakfast at half-past-eight till nine, then worked till half-past-twelve, and then we started again at quarter-past-one until quarter-past-five. No breaks in between you know. And I used to have to sit on the floor to have my dinner, and I used to put my coat down and have a lay down and have forty-winks because I were tired. I were what they call a doffer then. When the spinners had finished we used to have to doff all the full reels off you see. It were, it were all right of a job. But I can remember my first week's wage, my mother kissing it! I can always remember her kissing it. Funny

*Rand's Mill, taken early this century. The Alhambra Theatre now stands on this site.*

that isn't it?"

*F. Born 1906*

"I left school at Christmas 1935 and by New Year's Day 1936 my sister had got me a job at Fred Ambler's, Dumb Mills. I went there as a winding lad, which means you bring bobbins for the winders. And you had what you called a share to look after. Mine consisted of about twelve winders. And I found at weekends, on the Friday when it was wage day, they all used to buy sweets and I used to get one off each of them, so it was in my interests to keep them filled with work. I used to fill their lockers and bring them skeps full of bobbins. And sometimes they'd ask me if I'd go to the Alhambra with them, they used to all go together in a big party. I was only fourteen then so it was quite an exciting night for me. The older girls used to tease you, as young lads going to work.

They'd say "Oh, things like that didn't happen," but they did. But once they'd given you this initiation you were passed, or classed as one of the boys. I remember this one girl asking me to hold her suspender button while she sewed it on, and I didn't know where to put myself. I was very embarrassed, as a fourteen year old in short trousers. I thought I had to do these things. You'd to do everything you were told."

*M. Born 1923*

"The mill lads used to pull my plaits. You see my hair was right long and my mother wouldn't let me have it cut. The lads used to pull my plaits and say "Penny stage," every time they passed me. My mother nearly killed me when I had a perm. "Oh," she said, "You look like a woman of the town!" She couldn't get over that you know."

*F. Born 1912*

"When I left Carlton my elder sister, she worked at Illingworth's mill in the spinning, and she asked for me and got me a job there — bobbin-ligging. It was the lowest possible form of work, in the spinning, for a youth, and the lowest wage. I actually got eleven shillings a week, of which I was allowed to keep a shilling for myself and ten shillings went in the home, which was a Godsend. And then the mill itself, well, I began to wonder whether I'd done the right thing, you know, in coming off school. I only worked twelve months at Illingworth's mill actually, but it was a terrible twelve months, although I mastered it. But the very atmosphere you know, you trotted off to work at seven o'clock in a morning and you went through those gates and, I don't know, the mill just seemed to **swallow** you.

You went through the door and you was overwhelmed at the roar of noise, and for about three days that was all you could hear was the roar in your ears. But after that you became part and parcel of it and you could talk quite normally. Although **you** didn't realise it, you were doing a lot of lip-reading. It was all built into the job."

*M. Born 1920*

"The first morning I started I was sweeping out. You'd to sweep under all the frames and pull all the fluff out. And my mother had made me have these corsets on, and I was crippled! So that night I put 'em under the mattress and went without them the next day and ooh, it was lovely! But when I come home she greeted me at the door and hit me over the head with the corsets. She said, "If you don't wear them, when you get to be a young woman you'll be like Mrs Grimshaw." Well it scared me stiff because Mrs Grimshaw was so fat she could hardly walk, but I didn't put 'em on no more and I've never worn one since."

*F. Born 1900*

"The only way you could get into the dyeing trade in my time was by starting as an errand boy. What you used to do, you used to go round every man that worked there with your book and pencil and ask him if he wanted anything bringing in. He used to write it down and he'd give you the coppers. You'd get him a chop, or a bit of steak, or some sausage or some cigarettes or a pennorth of snuff. 'Beef baht Bone' they called it in them days. And you used to get as much as you could at the Co-op, because you got it on your mother's number 6086 that were my mother's number, which used to boost the 'Divi' at the end of the quarter."

*M. Born 1910*

"If you wanted to go to the toilet you'd to go see the overlooker, and at the overlooker's desk there used to be what was known as a peg-board, and on this board there were names such as "Bobbin-ligger," "Taker-off," "Jobber lad," "Winding lad." Now if any of those holes were filled with the peg being put in, you couldn't go to the toilet, so that restricted you from 'laking' about in the toilets you see."

*M. Born 1921*

"I left school on the Friday night and I started at the mill on Monday morning, at John Cawthra's at Dudley Hill.

*Winders aged fourteen, Salt's Mill, Saltaire, 1930. Although wages were low, around ten shillings for a 55-hour week, parents wanted their children to start earning as early as possible.*

They had a welfare department. I mean this is in the 1930's, but they never paid no wage. We had to work over if they said so, it wasn't voluntary. They said, "You work over," you worked over! Now then this particular Sunday morning, it was a lady factory inspector in those days, she came in and she said, "Put your coats on and get off home." So we all went home, and when we went to the mill on Monday morning, when the gaffer came at 9 o'clock we'd all to go up into the welfare department. And he wanted to know whose parents had been complaining about us working over you see, and none of us knew, so he sacked the lot of us, and there were twenty of us."

*M. Born 1920*

"I said, "I've got sacked," so she gave me a clout and said,

"What for?" She didn't say, "Why have you been sacked?" first. I got the clout first and then she said, "What for?" And of course I told her. She said, "Wait till you dad comes home and we'll see." Anyway my father, when he came home from the mill at about half-past-five, she says, "He's gotten sacked." And he says, "I know, I've heard about it on the grapevine. But when I've had me tea," he says, "we'll go and see George Wilkinson on Tong Street," that was a gaffer at a firm called Popplewell and Ingham's, which was later Pepper-Lee's and later became part of Salt's of Saltaire. Anyway when he'd had his tea, he put his cap on, he says, "Come on," and we walked on to Tong Street, which is possibly three or four miles — went to see George. George had heard that us lads had gotten sacked you see, and my father says to him, "Have you a job for him?" so George says, "Well aye." My father says, "Well wait a minute," he says, "he isn't coming to waste his time, I want him into a trade." So George said, "Well, what do you want him to be?" "I want him to be an overlooker." So George said, "Well I can do that," he says, because Jack Townend, who was an apprentice at that time, would have been out of his time, by the time I'd been there twelve months, so he said, "If he sets his stall up, he can start." So I started the following morning you see."

*M. Born 1920*

"Well of course ten shillings was fifty pence, in this present currency and it was, it was good money. But in June 1939 I had an accident, broke my leg playing football. I was keen on football and it was for the work's team, but I had a letter saying, 'In consequence of your absence from the office, we are instructed to reduce your salary to six-and-three pence per week, commencing the 1st June. We trust you will make a speedy recovery and should be glad to know when you are eligible to return to your duties. On your return to the office, you will of course resume your normal salary.' And Mr Norris, the accountant at Courtaulds, signed that. Well, you can understand that I certainly recovered quickly. To be reduced to six-and-three per week, and I went back to work on crutches, to make sure I got back to my ten shillings per week. Very happy times really."

*M. Born 1924*

"My mother approached a neighbour who worked in the burling and mending at Lister's, and she says, "My daughter's leaving school" (we were always daughters and sons, they were very formal actually). And she said, "I want her to get into a good job, something that's going to last her." Well this lady was in burling and mending and I didn't want to go into burling and mending because to me they were all old ladies. I wanted to go into the cone-winding where my sister worked, where there was a little bit of life going on you see. Anyway, I didn't go in either. Everybody thought I was very lucky because I managed to get into the knitting wool department which was supposed to be a quite posh job. It was Lister's Lavenda and if people had run short they sent a scrap of wool and you would send maybe one or two skeins of wool. It was in a hank, not in balls like they sell them today. Then I was moved into the place where they packed the wool up, twenty bundles at a time. There was a machine, a big wheel that you wound round, I used to feel like the captain of a ship — it actually pressed them so you could make it into a reasonable sized bundle."

*F. Born 1924*

"They always wanted doffers in the mill. And when you went into the mill this doctor would come, you'd be taken into the office, you'd be examined and as long as you could breathe you were fit to work in the mill. Nobody got rejected! Well I was in the doffing quite a while and then I got shoved down into the scouring department."

*M. Born 1914*

X

"I left St. John's School in Ashley Street when I was 14. My father approached Mr. Selka whom he met at the Synagogue and Mr. Selka interviewed me and said he would bear it in mind and two or three weeks afterwards

*Young woman spinner with doffer. Boys, even if they started work in spinning, normally moved on to such jobs as sorting, scouring, combing or mechanical work. Fison's, Burley-in-Wharfedale, 1905.*

sent for me. In those days Mr. Selka had a small office on Union Street and he had one employee, a girl, and I was the new office boy. I started on March the 3rd 1918 at fifteen shillings per week and in three or four months it was raised to eighteen shillings.

I started at nine till six o'clock but many times it was long after that because when we'd finished I had to take the mail, registered mail, ordinary mail and so on to the General Post Office.

In the September when I started evening classes at Carlton School I went straight from the Post Office to my classes, which in those days started at seven o'clock to nine o'clock, then come home, have my tea and do my homework, so it was quite a bind."

*M. Born 1904*

*Spinning shed, 1948.*

"I got well in at the Y.M.C.A. in my youth. We used to play table tennis in front of the altar, but come Sunday night when Sir George Garnett came with his groups we all had to stop and have a service. And before I even left School George Garnett did say to me, "You come down and see me lad, you can have a job in my mill," and that was the biggest mill in the area at that time. But because my family had always gone to Fisher's Mill, then **I** was destined for Fisher's Mill. I left on the Friday and started in Fisher's on the Monday. You got the impression that from say being eight years old your destiny had to be Fisher's Mill."

*M. Born 1934*

*Workers leave for lunch, Greenholme Mills, Burley-in-Wharfedale, c.1910.*

# WOMEN IN THE MILL

"I paid her thirty shillings to learn to weave"

*Weaving of all-wool serge at Greenholme Mills, Burley-in-Wharfedale, 1905.*

"When we worked in the mill we used to look at the office girls, I mean they had office girls in the mill, and we used to think they were toffee-nosed, you know. We used to think, "Oh, stuck-up things." And then when I came to work in an office, I remember an argument with some of the girls at work, I think somebody had been to the counter or something, and there was some comment made, "Well she was only a mill girl." Well, I just turned round and said "What's wrong with mill-girls?" "Well they're this, that and the other." I said "Well, I was a mill girl." "You what?" I said, "I was a mill girl and they're just people like you, they're just doing a job." I said, "And I'll tell you what, they're working a damn sight harder for their money than what you're working for yours."

*F. Born 1924*

"Then I decided I'd like to learn to weave, so the Boss

said, "Well go and see if you can get one of the weavers to take you to learn and you'll have to pay her thirty shillings." So I went round and nobody wanted a learner. I got to the last pair of looms but one and I said to her, "Will you take me to learn to weave?" So she said, "Oh I don't know, I don't think I want to be bothered with a learner." So I said, "Oh, don't say no. I've been all round and nobody will have me. You'll get three pound." I said, "The Boss had told me that I've to pay thirty shillings and they'll pay thirty shillings." So she said, "Oh go on then I'll take you." So I went to learn weaving there and then. After that I went on one loom on my own. Well you had what you earned then. If you'd to wait for a warp for a couple of days you didn't earn anything."

*F. Born 1903*

"If you didn't get there for seven you were 'quartered'. Well one day I had a 'quarter' and I couldn't go in, I **daren't,** so I went to another firm across the road and started there."

*F. Born 1912*

"There was no conversation as such and it was so noisy you learned to lip read, and you could speak to each other over the top of the frames. But if you were caught talking too much you were told about it in no uncertain terms. But you had to do something. Fortunately for us the rhythm of the belt and the machinery would start off a song, and it would create into another one and we would sing nearly all day long."

*F. Born 1924*

"We'd no wash-basins, they used to have a bucket of water in the middle of the aisle with a tablet of soap, and you'd to wash your hands in there. Some of the young boys would think nothing of getting a dead mouse and dropping that in, and there'd be ladies screaming all over the place."

*F. Born 1924*

"What we did with the overlooker, Duke Lightowler, we made a parcel up. We put orange peel, mucky bobbins, mucky sweepings-up, and made a lovely parcel and wrote on it 'To our Beloved Overlooker from his Doffers.' Well then he got hold of it and looked at it you know, he's looking right slyly around him, and he crept out and went into the men's toilet. When he come out he shied the bobbins at us, orange peel, apple conks, banana skins. Anyhow he were, he were a lovely overlooker, we loved him."

*F. Born 1904*

"The women would tell the overlookers off if they thought they were playing around and didn't come to mend their machine because, of course, it was losing them money if their machine was idle."

*F. Born 1928*

"When I worked at Mason's there were no men in the spinning, only the overlooker and his assistant. I remember coming out on strike once. How it happened they would put all the bobbins on, but then they put a little thing in the wheels at the end, which speeded the machine up. So we were having to work twice as fast, and they weren't giving us any extra money. We were running about like **scalded hens**!! As we got to that end, this end was coming out, and we were at it all the time. And we didn't have a rest in between!

So we decided that if we were working like this we should have some extra money for it. I might have been the one who asked the overlooker, and he said he would see what they said, but they said "No." We'd have only had about threepence at the end of the week. I mean it weren't a lot. So we all downed tools and said we wanted to see the boss. He said we could either get on with it or get out!! So we walked out! And we went back the next day, but the manager came to me and said, "You're no longer working in here. You can go in the twisting." I said, "I don't like the twisting." He says, "You can take it or leave it." You see he thought I was a troublemaker, he as

*Spinners and overlookers, 1930s.*

much as said this. I thought, 'Well, I don't know what will happen when I get home. My mother will carry on.' But she didn't. She said, "You don't let anybody put on you. Fair's fair," and, you know, "Why should you get blamed for something you haven't done," you see.

When I went back for my wage they rang the manager to see if I could have it. I said, "Well, I've worked for it." Anyway, he came down, and he said "What are you doing?" I said, "I aren't doing anything yet, but," I said, "you can't take my hands away from me. I'll get a job somewhere." So he said, "Well look, I'll let you have a job in the burling and mending. Will you go?" They knew, he **knew** that he was in the wrong. But the burling and mending was the elite thing, so I said, "All right, I'll give it a try." And they did get their increase after all that!"

*F. Born 1904*

"I wove a lovely piece of a crêpe de chine for one of the Foster's children, it was a sample. The piece-end had to be cut off because it was oily, and I asked if I could take it home because they'd asked me especially if I would have it on my loom. And without being pompous, I was proud of my work. I kept that piece-end for years and years."

*F. Born 1908*

"At dinner time, we'd no canteens. You ate your fish and chips sat on the window bottom where you did your work. When you were children you could only have either a bag of chips or a cake, but when you started bringing a wage in you could get fish and chips and that was part of growing up, you know, you felt part of a wage earning family."

*F. Born 1924*

"I tipped up my wage to my mother until I got married when I was twenty-two."

*F. Born 1924*

"Oh it was a very well run firm really. The bosses would come round and smile at you, look at the work. You **never** spoke to them. If you'd any grumbles about the yarn or the wages or anything like that it all had to go up through the overlooker, to the under-manager, from the under-manager to the manager and then the manager had to go literally cap-in-hand to the boss of all who paid the wages. And then eventually it would get back to you, and by that time that work would have been finished that you were complaining about, so really the strategy was excellent."

*F. Born 1924*

"There were one fellow, and we used to call him "Touchy," because every time he come reckoning to look at the box, he used to be touching your behind. And I remember one time I were on the box, and we used to warn each other when he used to be coming. They all used to say "Watch him with Hilda." And of course this day, I didn't know he were on, and I were doing something with my machine, and he come and put his hand right across my bottom. So I turned round, I picked a bobbin up and hit him with it! So they had me in the office for it. So, the gentleman that was over the overlookers, he asked me what I'd hit him for. So I told him. I said "When he stops touching my arse, I'll stop hitting him with bobbins."

*F. Born 1927*

"I went into the Roving shed at Moorside Mill when the war broke out (WW2). It had about fifty frames in it and there would be about a dozen girls. We had what they call four frames to look after and we were on piece work and that was hard, really hard, because your frame had eighty-eight bobbins on the bottom and twice as many on the top, so you had a hundred-and-seventy-six bobbins to lift up empty and a hundred-and-seventy-six bobbins to lift up full, and when they'd run through you'd all those to lift down. Now even if you'd been there a long time you couldn't earn any more because you could only work as fast as you could work, you know. And it was very heavy work in the drawing, because it used to have great big gill box and we'd to hoist those about, you know, the wool that came from the combing in great big drums. It had to be fed through rollers to make it longer and thinner, and put onto big bobbins. And then those big bobbins were put on a machine and run through and put on smaller bobbins, and then we got those to run even smaller and finer. And each time it's drawn out longer and thinner on more and more bobbins, and from there it went to the spinning. There were great big leather belts that used to go round and if you got cross with your machine, which you did, you used to slam the rod on and then slam it off and the belts used to crack. If you did that too many times the belt used to break and then you'd to go tell the overlooker, and he'd play 'pop' because he had to come and mend it with staples. I once saw a girl have her clothes ripped off her by a belt that had snapped. I think it caught her legs and the fact that it had wound her clothes round the flyers had cushioned it, but it had pulled all her clothes off, literally torn them down the back and nobody heard

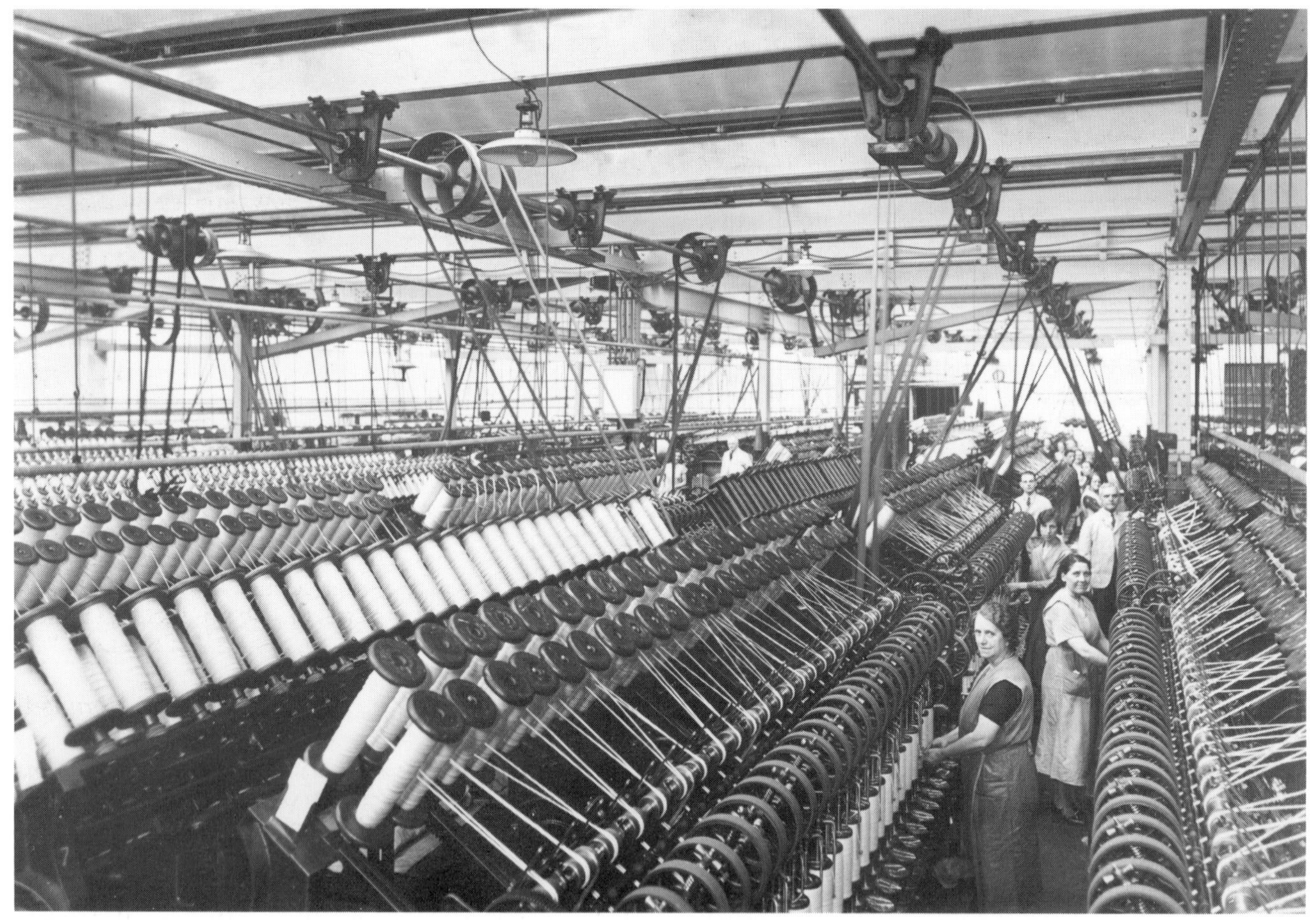

*Roving department of a Bradford mill, 1930s.*

her screaming, it was so noisy in there. I always remember because she had green bloomers on underneath. I've a knuckle that's deformed through catching it on one of the flyers. They used to fly round at a terrific rate. I once got a great big black splinter down my nail, it must have been off the bins where they kept the bobbins. There was no first aid room, and the first aid man worked in the boiler room. When I went and told him he put his hand in his pocket and got out a dirty penknife, flicked it open, got hold of my thumb and he just cut my nail in a great big 'V' and worked it out. He put me a bit of iodine on and said, "Right you can go back to work now."

If you wanted to go to the toilet you used to say to somebody, "Mind my box for five minutes," and if she was busy your box had got into a mess when you got back. And if you got in what they called a 'mullock' and all your ends went down, you'd to start there and pull all your ends up again. And that lost you money, because your box wasn't running. I used to go down the middle of my box and scream, it used to get on my nerves that much. And on a Friday morning we had those boxes to clean, and that meant crawling on your hands and knees at the back of your box with a piece of waste and wiping all the spindles to take all the black grease off. We used to go home at lunch-time with black grease up to our elbows and the smell used to get everywhere. You'd to come home at night and have a bath and wash your hair before you went out. And yet there were women who had gone in as young girls, and they were in their early sixties and they'd never known anything else.

Our overlooker was an old devil, he really was. He was grey-haired, hunch-shouldered and he used to walk round and if he caught you sitting on your waste can, you used to have a can at the end of your box to put the waste in, if he caught you sitting down for five minutes he used to swear at you. "Get up you lazy bugger and get on with some work." And that might have been the first time you'd sat down all day. You were on your feet from half-past-six in the morning to half-past-six at night. So you used to have to keep your eye out for him."

*F. Born 1924*

"I went and got a job at Woolworth's as a Saturday girl. We worked Saturday mornings at Whitehead's then and I think we finished at quarter-to-twelve. And I'd to run home, up Dick Lane, have my dinner, get washed and changed and be right up at Woolworth's for one o'clock.

I worked there from one o'clock till nine and it was five shillings. If you were on short time you could ask to go in all day Saturday. It was ten shillings for all day. I went there in the first place because we only got one-and-six spending money, and if we wanted to go dancing, we could only afford to go once. So five shillings was like a fortune."

*F. Born 1908*

"I used to go home when I'd been in the weaving all day and wash for eight of us, with a tub and a rubbing board and a big wringer. They were all to rub, and twine and poss."

*F. Born 1924*

"Money was very tight, so I went back to work when she was six weeks old. I only got twenty three shillings a week and I was paying eight shillings for her minding. I used to run home at breakfast time, breast feed her, run back to work, then come home at dinner time and feed her again, and this is how it was."

*F. Born 1902*

"I went to work at Smith's up Allerton in 1936. But what happened, there was a recession, and they were getting rid of the married women. That was the attitude in that day and age. So then I went to Wood's up Allerton Road because I could twist or wind or do anything like that. I would run down home at dinner time, see to the children's dinner, snatch a sandwich walking about, then run back to work. You see I always made a hot meal at tea-time."

*F. Born 1903*

"This girl that worked with me was in the Francis Laidler pantomine, and they let her go out of the mill every Wednesday for rehearsals, and when she came back at Thursday she used to show us all what they'd been doing. Well this here day we all had to put our hands on her shoulder and it was one, two, three, (SINGS) "If you see a field where grass is blue and everything looks good to you, you're in Kentucky sure as you're born." We all danced up this back alley and suddenly they're all disappearing, and when I looked I'm right facing the old man, the overlooker, and he said, "Now then, what's thou doing?" I said "I'm practising for the pantomine Fred," he said "Well thou's all next week to practice," he said, "Thou's sacked."

*F. Born 1908*

"I could only afford one perm a year so I used to be in the perm club at work. We used to pay sixpence a week. There were so many people in the club, and you each drew a number out and went for your hair perming that week. If you were lucky and drew a low number you got your perm before you'd paid for it. And there was a lady who walked to work with us and she ran what we called a 'diddleum.' That was how you saved money for your holidays."

*F. Born 1921*

"After the war, (WW2) I went straight back into the drawing. But I did work in the combing shed for a long number of years. It was a filthy place, horrible really, because in those days you had shaft belting, and belts breaking and if you weren't careful you got a smack in the face with them! The toilets weren't very good either. They were those toilets with a wood seat and a hole in, and you could see right down to the bottom. We had a long trough with a brass tap every so far to wash your hands. The soap they made themselves in long bars. The overlooker used to cut it off in chunks and send the jobber lad round with it. You all had your own piece of soap but it was as hard as pot and you couldn't get a lather with it. There were no towels in them days, you just had what we called a mill cloth, you put it over a can to dry. There was a boiler for mashing your pot of tea but nothing else, and the lighting was very poor."

*F. Born 1921*

"When I worked at Illingworth's I had twins, but they died. November 1948 it was. I was due in March. You could only get money for six weeks before your baby was born and as it was my first and I was living with my mother, I wanted the money. I were putting bobbins up at work, weighing, carrying bobbins and I started having these pains. I left work at five-o'clock and I had the first baby at half-past-six and I didn't know I was having twins. I had the little girl at home on the rug. I didn't know what to expect. The water bag come away and I didn't know what it was. I just says to my husband, "My insides coming away, go fetch my mother." Then the doctor came and said "There's another one there." Anyway, they had to get an ambulance and take me to St. Luke's. It was thick of fog, one of the ambulance drivers had to walk in front to see us up Park Road. And I'd all my mill clothes on, on the labour table. Afterwards the overlooker said, "Never no more." But you see it learnt them a lesson that they hadn't to keep anybody on heavy boxes when they were having babies."

*F. Born 1927*

"And I think the reason women got phased out was that it was easier to put men on Continental shift working, four days on and four days off. You see it's harder for a woman if she happens to be married and has children. Most women needed that weekend at home to catch up with their housework and see to the children and everything else."

*F. Born 1919*

*Checking a delivery from Lumb Lane Mills, c.1920.*

# MEN IN THE MILL

"You thought it was your birthright"

"They had a time-keeper in a little office by the mill gates known as the Penny Hole, and at that time, in Wilsden they started at half-past-six in the morning. The mill gates were closed and anyone coming late were forced to go through the Penny Hole and the man there would make a note of it and there was a penny taken off your wage. And the same thing happened if you were back late at meal times. Now the spinners earned eleven and six a week so if you were late a few times it was reducing your wage quite a bit. But they did change that procedure in later years."

*M. Born 1896*

"Well you'd have Mason's, C. F. Taylor's and Salt's, but although they all had a seven o'clock start they had various methods of letting you know what time it was. Salt's had a buzzer. Now Mason's, they had a bell that used to go at five-to-seven and seven o'clock, and then the gates were locked. There was a chap there on the 'Penny Hole' as they called it, just inside the gates and if them gates were shut you were 'quartered' and had to go back at breakfast time. There was only one bloke who got away with it and he did it two mornings in one week. He knew just where the coal was stacked inside the mill yard and he'd heave his bike over the wall onto the coal, and climb over and come in that way."

*M. Born 1917*

"In that mill there was an initiation thing for all young men. And they used to chase you at dinner times, all the lasses in the mill; it was the known thing, even the manager knew, everybody knew. And they used to chase all the new young fellows that came into the mill and get them down and oil their private parts. Me being a wild one it took them about a month to get me. But then, everybody else was done the same so it didn't really matter, but it was a bit embarrassing. And my mother was in the same mill so she didn't really worry too much because she'd probably chased a few in her time."

*M. Born 1934*

*Wool Sorters outside Taylor's sorting shed off Sunbridge Road, c.1910.*

"They're a very strange set of people, woolsorters. There's a couple of words that are only ever used in sorting that are never used anywhere else, and one of them's 'shoiling,' and that's when they're talking about holidays and you have a cheap holiday by staying at a relative's house. The head sorters used it. "Oh you're going shoiling." I don't know how to spell it, it's just a word. And the other word is 'dog-arse' and it means to contradict somebody, and I've only ever hear that word by sorters."

*M. Born 1944*

"The taker-off in the wool-sorting was another name for the foreman woolsorter. The taker-off used to go to work in a bowler hat, the wool-sorters wore flat caps. At work they all wore a 'brat.' It's a long, protective garment with blue and white stripes, which went from the neck to the ankles and tied at the back with two tapes. We all wore those. But the taker-off would make sure the sorters were putting the right qualities together. That's how you get your botany wools, your crossbred and all these other qualities."

*M. Born 1925*

"Fourteen I was, when I started work at Lister's in the spinning. I started as a bobbin ligger, that were, you know, putting bobbins on machines. And I graduated from that to a doffer, and from a doffer to a jobber lad. I worked there eight year in the spinning, and then I got too old for the job and got finished. You see I kept asking for a rise, and one day the foreman said he were dammed well fed up with me asking for a rise, and two days later I got finished! I don't know what I got finished for but that was the main thing, because a couple of days after I got a letter from the dole. I'd to go down to Nelson Street and appear in front of a Court of Referees. So I went down and I walked in this room and there were about six men sat round a long table, and they were asking me questions so I told them what the foreman had said.

So the Chairman of the Board, he said, "Well I think it's a case of this man's got too old for the job and they've put somebody younger in for less wage." And I'd no trouble getting my dole then, you see. If they'd gone against me I'd have had to wait six weeks before I got anything, and I were married and I had a youngster, a little girl."

*M. Born 1913*

"After the strike when Mr William sent for me, he said "Now then, there's a share of looms in that shed, do you want them or don't you?" "Well" I said "I can't follow a share of looms, I've only had a year-and-a-half apprenticeship." "Nonsense," he says, "I can learn a man to overlook in twelve months." And I hadn't an answer, you see I'd either to take the job or be out of work. "Well" he says, "you'll be on a fixed rate at a pound a week less than the overlookers are getting." He says "Always remember this my boy, hard work doesn't kill no-one." Well I'm not lying, I were oiling looms of a Sunday! The full-man couldn't follow them so what chance had I, an apprentice? Later on, there was another reduction. I think it were about five shillings they were knocking off and I always remember him sending for me. "Now then" he said "I won't reduce your money, so" he says "I've given you a five shillings rise haven't I? Now get in there and show your appreciation." Good old days, eh?"

*M. Born 1911*

"They used to have their own little "Sick Clubs" there, in fact I used to be secretary of one called the Mechanics Sick Club. There were various little schemes going which might have been illegal, I don't know, but you paid about threepence a week, and if anybody was off sick they'd let me know and I'd put it in my little book, and take them this fifteen bob or whatever it was, but that's about all there was, you know."

*M. Born 1921*

"The conditions in the dyehouse were terrible, **terrible.** It was full of steam. When all the vessels got on the boil you couldn't see in front of you, but you accepted all these terrible things because you thought it was your birthright. And when you first went in the stench was intolerable. You used to think, "I'll never get used to this," but within a day or two you couldn't smell anything, you know, the acids, the colours and whatever. It was all manual labour. The pieces used to come in in the "grey," untreated, from the customer and they were sorted out and marked up to

*Dyehouse at Salt's Mill, Saltaire, c.1920.*

what they had to have done to them, the finish, the shade and everything. Then they went on to the crabbing, steaming and then into the scouring where they were scoured between rollers with textile soap and then washed off and sorted into their respective shades, whatever the customer wanted. Then from the dyeing they went to the tentering. They were stretched out on pins and went through these huge ovens, and when they came out at the other end they were bone dry."

*M. Born 1910*

"I was six years in the dye-house at Lister's 'till I got sacked. I were twenty one then. What happened, it was all thick steam and there was me at one side of a machine, and this Arthur Bowser at the other, and we were throwing 'sops' at one another, you know, wet paper, old cloth or ought. So I threw it and it hit the manager. He came straight across, never saw me through this thick steam, and he sacked Bowser. Well I wasn't a hero by any means, it would have come out who'd thrown it so I went in and confessed. He say, "Well it's good of you to confess." So I got the sack!"

*M. Born 1906*

"We had a lad with us, they called him Stanley, he got killed in the Navy during the war. But I remember Stanley one day was going for the dinners and Jimmy Snowden, one of the overlookers had told him to bring him two penn'orth of polony and post his coupon, that was his football coupon. And when Stanley came back he'd posted the polony and brought him the coupon back! Jimmy made him go and get Goldboroughs, which was the post office-cum-sweet shop, to open the post box and get his polony out, and bring it back to the mill. Now when pieces came out of the loom they had to be folded, and then these pieces had to go to the floor above, to the mending and they used to be loaded on a cart and taken by crane. You had to run up the stairs, pull the cart in and unload it. Well this day the overlookers were watching Stanley and they said to him, "Stanley, you don't want to be going up them steps, get in the cart and we'll pull you up." So he gets in the cart and they pulled him half-way up between the floors and left him. There was Stanley swinging in the crane, outside in the mill yard, shouting for help. The gaffer came, looks at him, wanted to know who'd done it. There was hell-to-do! They were up to all them tricks. You'd go to get your coat on to run for the tram, and you'd find the weavers had sewn your sleeves up, or you'd go for your jock out of your pocket and it would be missing. They'd pinched it and eaten it!"

*M. Born 1920*

"It was quite common to have another job going to supplement your income. Same as fellows used to bring chocolate to sell and cigarettes, things like that. You used to get penny bars or Frys or five Woodbines at twopence a time. And you used to get it on 'tick' and pay at the weekend."

*M. Born 1913*

"Having a bet was popular in the mills. Mind you it were illegal, it were before there were any betting shops. At that period there was an opening from the recreation ground right down to the mill, and at Beamsley Street corner there was a greengrocers. Well all the lads used to congregate there.

He got done once or twice by the police did the bookie, aye, same as my mother used to take bets for him and all you see. One Saturday the police walked into my mother's, and of course she had some bets on the table. She were waiting for him coming. Well, she were in a right state were my mother because they took her down to the Town Hall, and I mean nothing like that had ever happened to her before. She got fined but the bookie paid it. She turned it in after that, she wouldn't have no more to do with it."

*M. Born 1913*

"The biggest part of a spinning mill was female labour, and being only young the warping department comprised of a lot of ladies that were a lot older than I was, and they decided to make my life hellish misery, because I was only a kid. So I had to think up a plan of how I could make them pay the respects to me that was due. So one overstepped the mark one day, so I sacked her there and then, and on her way out she asked to see the manager, and she told the manager what I'd done. And so he came up and saw me and said, "What have you sacked her for?" So I told him that I was the overlooker in that department, and I wasn't having her telling **me** what to do, **I** was telling **her**. "Oh," he said, "you did right." So she had to finish. So then it got me respect and I found out what overlooking was all about then, that you were in charge and it was **your** fault if anything did go wrong."

*M. Born 1922*

"If Mr Selka wanted a new cloth, he'd say, "Right, I want an 18 ounce pick-and-pick, or an 18 ounce gaberdine. Make a sample warp." Then he'd look at it, "No, do it again, a bit wider, a bit looser," whatever it was. When it

*Overlooker in Spinning Shed at Drummond's Mill, Lumb Lane, at the end of the First World War, 1918.*

was right he would have one piece made, and when it came into the warehouse he'd cut 6 suit lengths off. Then he'd go round various places in the mill giving them out. He'd say, "Here I want you to make a suit of that, wear it continuously for 6 weeks and then I want to see it." When the suits came back we had them dry cleaned and looked at them. If they were okay we would start production, if not we'd start again. That is the way to run a business."

*M. Born 1903*

*Mechanic's shop in a spinning mill, c.1935.*

# OTHER WORK IN THE MILL

"A fish and a penn'orth three hundred times"

"Now as a lad my job was to get there at about twenty to seven, and I'd to go round and light all the gases, so that people coming in for seven o'clock could see in. And to do this I had a little torch made out of wick and a canister filled with paraffin, and this was on a long piece of wire, with a hook on the top to pull the gas chain you see, to pull the gas on, then I used to light it. I didn't smoke in those days, and the boss used to give me a box of 'Tiger matches.' These were right big matches, and he used to give me tu'pence to get my matches, when I required them. And I went to the mill this particular morning and there were no matches. Somebody had pinched them! Of course everybody was coming to work then, they were coming in, in the dark and they were falling over the carts and one thing and another, and there was hell to do! Anyway at nine o'clock, the gaffer comes flying through and his head's going round looking for me, and I'm hiding, watching for him. Anyway, he saw me, "Come here," he says. So I went to him, took me in the office, "How is it the lights weren't on this morning?" I said, "Somebody pinched my matches," Well he gave me a right clout, "I'll give thee somebody pinched my matches," he says. "This will teach you, not to let somebody pinch 'em. You should have put them somewhere where they don't know where they are. Anyway," he says, "here's another tuppence, go and get some matches from the shop." So on the Friday he took tuppence off me for the matches, that I'd lost you see. So I made sure in future that nobody pinched my matches."

*M. Born 1920*

"My mother worked at Shaw's for a short space of time, but she worked in the cookhouse. All these things that the errand lad used to buy, like chops for one man, sausages for another man, things like that, were all taken to the cookhouse, and there were two women that worked there and stayed while about three o'clock in the afternoon. They did the breakfasts, and the men, they used to take their bacon and eggs and all like that. There was nothing provided. They used to have to take all their own and these two women, and my Mum was one of them, they used to cook these fellows' breakfasts and their dinners."

*M. Born 1910*

"There were twenty-eight of us all told on the office staff, invoice clerks and what-have-you, the office staff on one floor, as I said, the packing-house down in the basement. When I was up-to-date I used to nip down and help Bill. Mr Selka caught me one day. "What are you doing down here?" "I'm just helping Bill," because I used to get my muscle up for playing Rugby, you see, chucking pieces about. "Is your work up to date?" "Yes, sir." "Right. You must not come down here unless you have no work to do upstairs." Then when the warehouse became really busy they used to send for us. "Will you go down in the packing shop, Fred?" I was thrilled to bits, packing cases, sewing bales, and if you weren't too careful, you could get the sewing needle through the pieces as well as stitching the canvas."

*M. Born 1910*

"You could walk up to Lister's then any time and get some sort of a job. So I went and saw this chap and he says, "I've got a nice little job if you fancy it, in the reed making shop." Of course I didn't know anything about reed-making. So he said, "It's a good job, a skilled job." So I said, "Okay I'll give it a whirl." I'll never forget when I went in that place; two areas as big as football fields with about six hundred and sixty looms, all shuttle looms, which make a lot of row you know. Deafening! Anyway this shop that we had was a little bit away from the weaving, sort of on its own, and this chap, Willie Penny, said, "Now then" he said, "You're going to work with me and I'm going to show you what to do." He said he didn't want cheek, and I said "Fair enough" like. And he said, "Whatever you do, be **tidy**. A tidy workman, a tidy job." It was a proper apprenticeship in those days, it isn't now, I don't think. I mean, we used to have to roll our own wire, do all the workings out.

There were about six machines for rolling the wire, then there were polishing machines, and then there was

*Transporting materials from one part of Manningham Mills to another.*

the reed-making machine itself. The reeds for light jobs like warping were dipped in pitch to give them body. Weaving reeds are a bit more substantial, they're soldered. They're all worked out to the width of cloth you want, and the number of ends or threads that you are going to need through. Obviously if you only needed four hundred threads in fifty inches wide, say, your reed is going to be a lot coarser than it would if you wanted two thousand threads in the same width.

People came from all over the mill to sniff this tank of pitch, like the old tar wagons that they used to have on the road that they used to hold their babies over when they had whooping cough. Funnily enough I can't ever recall having a bad cold there, I don't know whether that were owt to do with it. When I got demobbed in 1946 they'd stopped making the reeds at Listers, so now it was just a case of repairing them all the time. But it's an awful strain on your eyes, especially if you're getting these right fine ones. You've got to straighten them all up, and I mean they used to drop tin pots and all sorts in them and bash them to bits, and you had them all to straighten so that they didn't show any marks when they were weaving. Actually it's a lot harder repairing them than it is making them.

But we had some great fun when I first went there. I remember there weren't flush toilets as there are today. All the toilets were in a line and a sort of channel ran underneath with the water running through all the time, you know, a continuous flow of water, and us kids used to make paper boats and set them on fire and float them down these channels, and then the gaffer he'd be chasing us all over the place. I remember one chap there used to have a bit of bent wire and he used to fasten big lumps of mouldy old cheese on these bits of wire and anybody that was walking past he just used to hook it onto their back.l I've seen people walking about for hours like that.

I remember one day they had a fire, not a serious fire, but the fire brigade came, and all these blooming firemen were walking about with a tail of a big lump of horrible smelling cheese!

When I were a lad there was this narky old fellow, he was always shouting at you, right nasty. He worked at a bench, cleaning reels, right mucky job it was. Well one of the blokes got a kipper that was going off, and he nailed it under his bench. It was there for days! You could smell it all over but this old chap was working away, he never noticed it at all, **never noticed it**, and it was blooming overpowering! Anyway at the finish-up the foreman made them take it off. One chap there, he come with a baby pig he'd bought somewhere and it got away in the weaving shed. He were chasing it all over. Another old chap, he used to sweep up, they called them "muckmen" in them days, and he was a brilliant violinist, bachelor he was, and a brilliant poet as well. You'd all sorts of characters."

*M. Born 1921*

"On one occasion we ran out of coal, and they bought a lot of tyres, and I remember we had to burn tyres for month after month, to keep the mill going, and everybody, all the local people in Havelock Street, Great Horton, Southfield Lane, they must have had a real difficult time, washing and cleaning their 'doorsteps' with these burning tyres."

*M. Born 1924*

"I thought working at Lister's as a bricklayer would be easier, working inside, no bother about being rained off, or having to fight all the time for a secure job, because I was turned fifty then and knew I would have to study my health a little bit. I was doing repairs to furnaces, chimney work and general repairs to their property, because they had other factories round about Bradford, and even in Burley-in-Wharfedale. It was often very hard, dirty work. In fact I suffered a rupture because of hard work I did at Lister's Mill. But you didn't face the elements like I'd done previously."

*M. Born 1911*

"Somebody burst into the office and said, "Mr Pogson, somebody's fainted, the girls are fainting in the weaving shed." And I dashed in, and one of the maintenance men, Arthur, he'd caught his fingers in the wheels, and they'd torn three of his fingers off, and they were on the floor, and there was blood on the floor and the girls were fainting. And somebody said, "You better get in there Mr Pogson, and pick those fingers up, otherwise it will stop the production," and I went, I'd to pick them up in an envelope and bring them back in the office. And in those days it was a matter of ringing up to see if they could put the fingers back on, but anyway I don't think it happened and think they'd to amputate. But there was no business of stopping the mill, or what have you, you'd to keep it going. And it was an export order for Japan ... it was rather difficult in those days."

*M. Born 1924*

"One of your jobs as a lad was to mash the tea for all the operatives and if there were a couple of hundred operatives, there might have been about twenty kids mashing the tea. And what you used to do, you used to go round and collect from them what we called 'mashings,' which your mother used to put up for you on a night. You know it would be a tea-spoon full of tea and two tea-spoons of sugar, wrapped in a bit of newspaper, you stuck that in your top pocket with a little bottle of milk and off you went.

You used to go to the fish shop at Fridays, always Fridays, and you might have wanted a fish and a penn'orth three hundred times, or a cake and chips a hundred and fifty times, and a fish on its own forty times and so on.

Popplewell's was a fair big mill. And of course we got commission from the proprietor of the fish shop for taking the business there, and them that gave us the most commission, that's the fish shop we used to go to. Of course as you got older and more kids came into the mill, they started having to do the menial tasks and you went on with your apprenticeship."

*M. Born 1920*

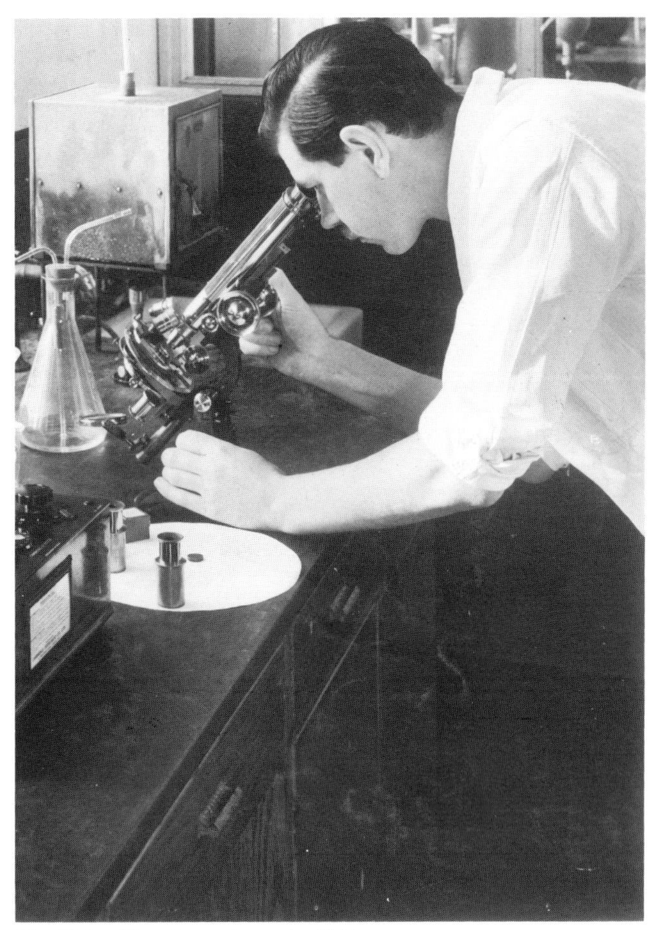

*Identifying fibres in wool sample, 1940s.*

"It was a small laboratory but it was at the heart of the mill, and it seemed very colourful and an interesting place to be. We tested at all stages from the raw fibre up to the finished material, or the finished knitting wool sample, or the finished piece of velvet.

It was all material that was being produced in the mill itself. It was a real hive of activity in there. I used to like to walk through the mill, although at first I got lost once or twice. The only place I didn't like going to much was into the dyehouse, because they were all men in there and they shouted out and had a joke with us. Well I was only sixteen at the time and a bit shy. But we had to collect and return samples to the leaders of the departments. It was mainly samples of wool, and knitting wool and yarn from cloth. We tested it for the strength of the individual strands. We tested it for humidity and to see if it had exactly the right amount of oil, water, to see if the dye was fast. We took apart samples of carpeting and we weighed each different colour, then we dried it out to see how much moisture content was in, and we did the same with samples of cloth and wool. It was very important to keep a high standard. We had a wearing machine, and we saw how many 'rubs' it needed to wear a hole in it and thus we were able to tell the quality of each particular item that we tested and we were able to send out a certificate with it, and I presume that they would send them out to the customers."

*F. Born 1939*

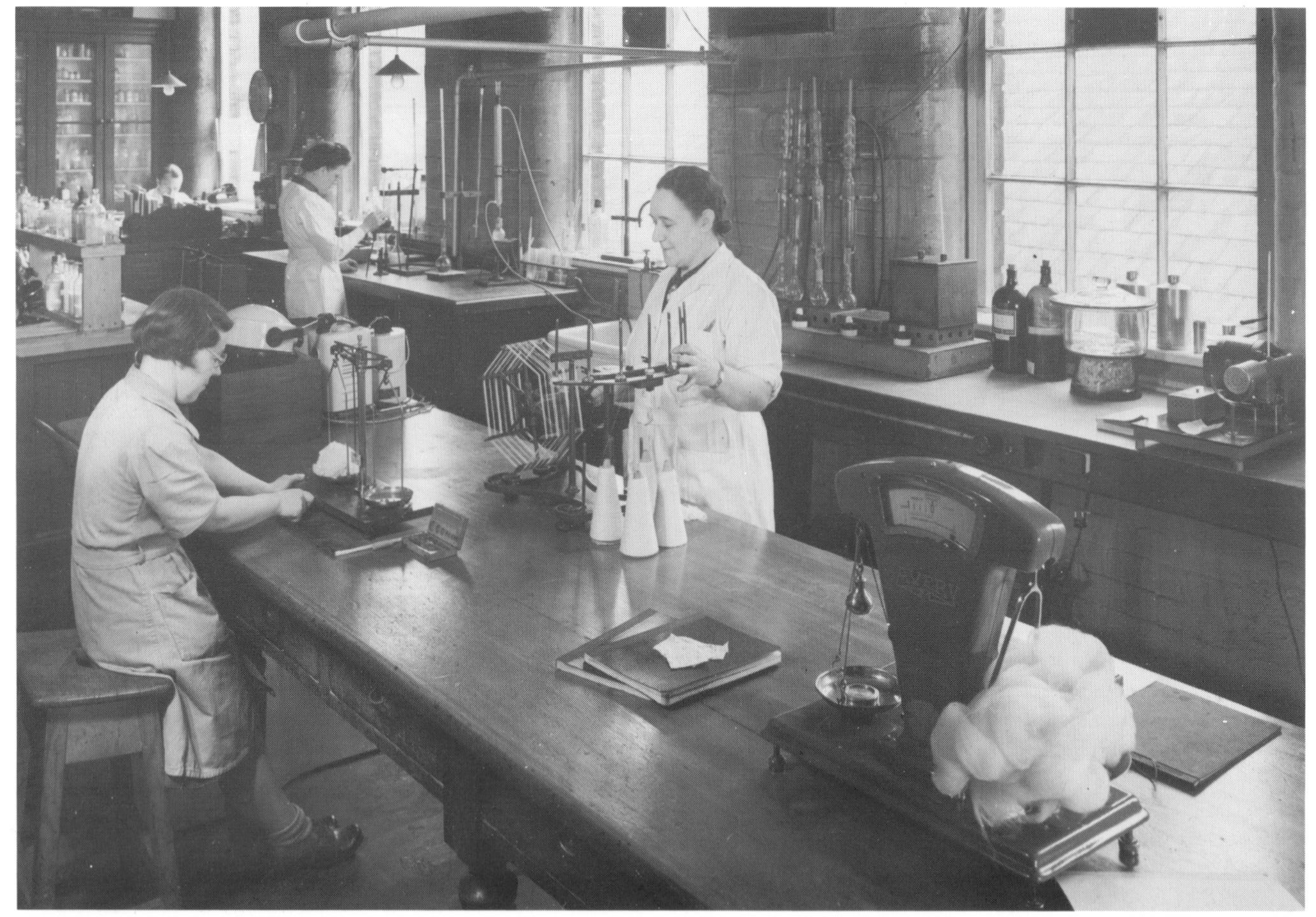

*Laboratory at Salt's Mill, Saltaire, 1949.*

"I joined this Welfare Department then, at Brigella Mills. All the mills were starting to improve their First Aid and Welfare facilities and Hield Brothers was no exception. And Miss Cragg, who was a S.R.N., she'd been brought in and she'd established this sort of surgery where people could go for cuts and bruises and help and general advice, and where you could visit people who were ill and take a real interest, sort of, in the workforce."

*F. Born 1929*

"There was one or two instances when the war broke out, the people who had to go and join the Forces had to leave their duties, and I had to take over more responsibility. I had to do ordering and purchasing and wages."

*M. Born 1924*

"I saw a thing in the paper about Woolcomber's Ltd.,

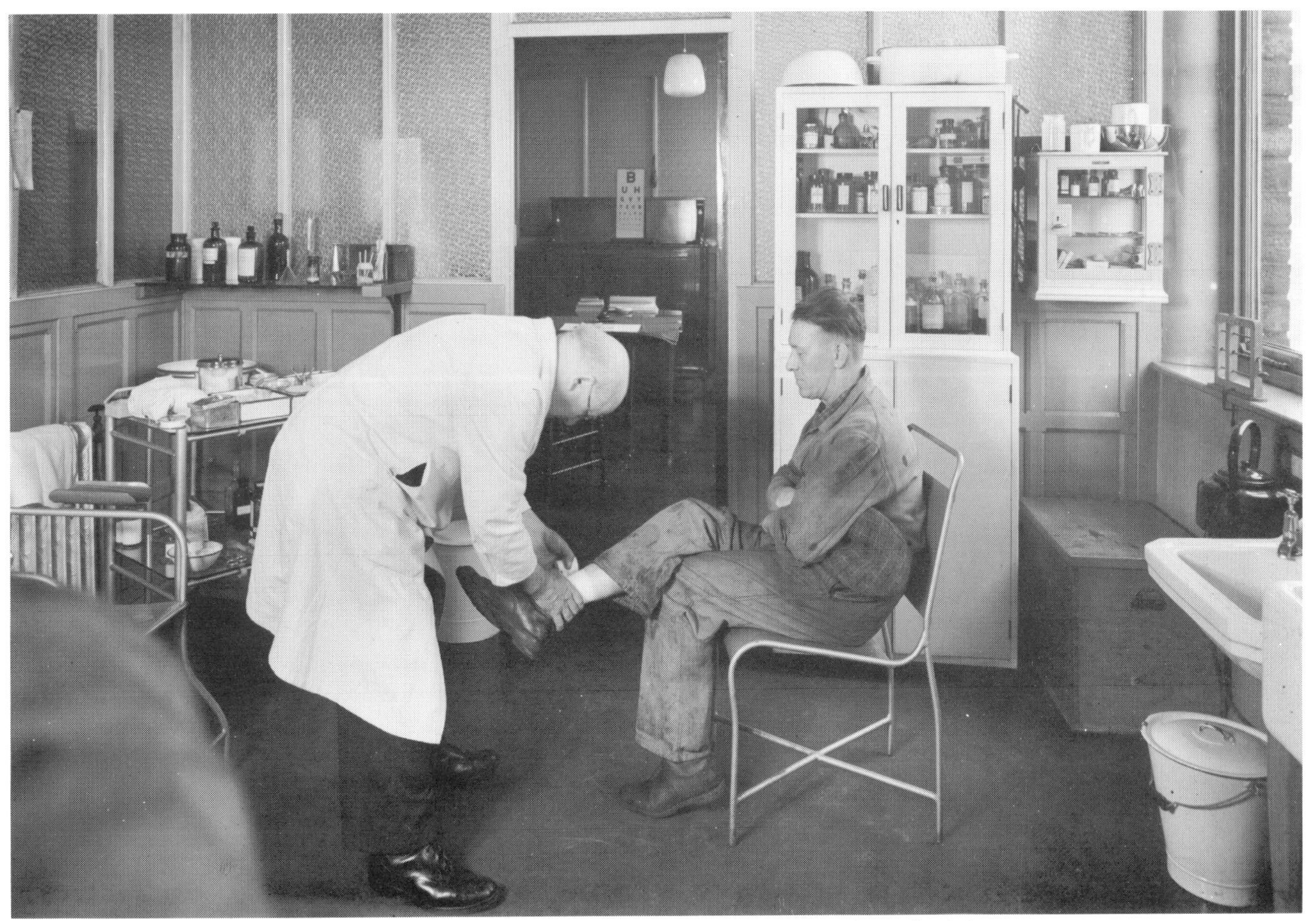

*Doctor's surgery, Salt's Mill, 1949.*

setting on junior clerks, and I went for an interview to their head office up Daisy Bank. There was a vacancy in their transport department. The first week, because it was a week in hand, I only got one pound fifty. That was 1960. After six years I was doing all the wages. Then what Woolcombers did, they brought 'time-and-motion' in and they brought the Transport department and the Central Workshop together, so I was offered a job as a warehouse clerk in the mill, which was a step down really. I worked longer hours and overtime, which I hadn't done in the other job but it was a lot bigger wage."

*M. Born 1944*

"There were two engines at Ambler's, 'Susan' and 'Florrie.' They took their names from the owner's daughter. Friday afternoon they used to be polished like silver with crocus powder let down with paraffin. One had

*Loading yarn for export, Greenholme Mills, Burley-in-Wharfedale, c.1910.*

a rope drive, it had eight ropes on it. The other one, the five hundred horse power, that had big belts, one belt was fourteen inches wide. I used to take my turn at firing. There were five of us, two on nights, one in the engine room, one in the boiler house and one that oiled the shafting. The fire was kept going all the time except at Easter when we had to let the fires out for maintenance and de-scaling."

*M. Born 1896*

*Dominion Wool Disposals Ltd., 1948.*

# WORK OUTSIDE THE MILL

"Your humble servant, Fred"

"I learned to clip sheep by hand and I were fairly good even though I say it myself. At the time when I worked for Frank Sharpe, me and other lad that worked there, we'd to go at nights and weekends at clipping time and if we made a hundred pounds we'd made a lot of money between us. But now they are looking at making a thousand quid in a month or five week of clipping with a good clipping machine. But it's another income really, is wool. It depends what sort it is. There's a lot of difference in prices and quality of wool. Lowland wool is worth a lot more than this Swaledale wool, and Blackfaced wool isn't worth a lot because it's only carpet wool, that's sort of the lowest priced wool. But this finer wools that they can make into knitting wools, they can be worth half as much again as these more fibery wools."

*M. Born 1936*

"After about eighteen months I went to the Conditioning House because the wage there was much better. There it was mainly dealing with raw wool. Samples came in from all the big mills around Bradford and we had to test it for the width of the fibres. We had to look under the microscope and make our tests, and then work out an average for the width of fibres in each piece that we were testing. Again we had to test for oil and moisture content. We had to pick out what we called nips and burrs. They were the little bits of wool and fuzz and seeds and things which got into the raw wool. We also had a moth room there where we tested for the moth-proofing on certain materials. That was very hot. It had to be for the moths to survive. We put little samples of materials and wool in there and checked at regular intervals to see if they'd been eaten away. Probably each mill had its own small laboratory but the testing would vary enormously. At the Conditioning House the testing was more standardised. You see, Bradford was the centre for the wool industry and it was known all over the world, and the Conditioning House had been set up as a focal point of the wool trade. The Conditioning House was well-known world wide and a certificate from there was recognised all over the world."

*F. Born 1939*

"Leeds and Liverpool Canal Carrying Company had white boats with scrolls and fancywork. They came with wool and goods from Liverpool to Leeds. They had a big stable at Shipley with six or eight stalls. Sometimes, at weekends or holidays they'd put the horses in the field for two or three days, then you'd a job to round them up. There was one horse to each barge and you had that horse everytime. There were always two working on a barge, captain and mate, and it was the mate's job to mix the corn for the horses. Occasionally they'd slip an extra bag of corn into the cabin for the horse when the gaffers were away. There was a blacksmith at Baildon Bridge and another at Hargreaves Square. A boat horse was shod different to a cart horse. A cart horse had studs owing to the setts in the road. A boat horse had what they called a 'flat' shoe. They'd be pulling loads of forty to fifty ton. There used to be a "change horse" stable at Bingley Five Rise and another at Skipton Bridge.

Just before the war, about 1933 to 1938 there were a lot of wool fetched into Bradford, as though they knew there was going to be some trouble. By this time Bradford Canal had been closed so they built all these new warehouses on Wharfe Street at Shipley for the sole purpose of storing that wool.

There were little steamers which could pull thirty ton of coal in their own holds and fifty ton behind. There was the 'Patsy' and the 'Annie,' they were built for Shaw's dyehouse. The Canal Carriers' boats were always green, they mostly carried coal. C. F. Taylor's had their coal delivered straight off the canal into View Croft Road. Salts used to get most of their coal by boat. You tipped it onto the bank and this endless chain of overhead buckets came and tipped it down a chute to the boilers."

*M. Born 1908*

"We went to live with my grandparents in Preston Street, because my parents had started buying a house in Hoxton Street and couldn't keep up the mortgage. You see my father worked for the B.D.A. and although he was never out of work, they never sacked him, there was a tremendous amount of short time working. I mean

*Stables on Lawkholme Lane, Keighley, owned by Midland Railway, c.1930.*

sometimes they'd only work one day a fortnight, you know, something like that, and he had to sign on.

My grandfather was the horse feeder for Jabez Cole. It was right next door to Harrison's garage on the corner of Preston Street. The front of the house led into Preston Street, and the back door led into the back part where the stables were. My grandfather, who was brought up in an agricultural family, was asked by Jabez Cole to move from Norfolk to Bradford to look after these horses. He came up in 1912 and worked with the horses until 1946. They were all big cart-horse breeds, Suffolk Punches if he could get one. They had to be big to pull the coal! My grandfather would get up at half past five in a morning. I remember that because if I called out "Tea please" he'd bring me a cup, but he wouldn't wake me up to give me it. There was usually one horse and one man to each cart, but occasionally they'd put a two-horse team on if they had some special work. The men would take them down to

City Road coal 'drops' where all the coal trains came in, and they filled the wagons out of the 'drops' and weighed the whole thing on big scales. Then they took the loads to the mills and 'shuttered' them all out for the boilers, and they'd to do so many loads a day. While the horses were out of the way grandfather would clean out the stables, get deliveries of corn, take all the instructions. We'd plenty of places to play when the horses were out of the way. They just used to let us run about among the stables. Then when they came back at night he had to bed the horses down, and at ten o'clock he would do a round to see they were all right before everybody went to bed. They all had names. Sometimes he would go off to buy new horses and sometimes if they got sick they had to be shot. I suppose the horses became part of our lives.

In 1934 Jabez Cole went in with Smith, Parkinson and they moved the stables to Farnham Road. There was also a garage at the side of the stables because Mr Smith, who was one of the directors of Smith, Parkinson & Cole, garaged his car there. It was Marina Green, the "in" colour then. It was a lovely car. And we had a telephone, because even as a small child I could answer the telephone, and I would ask who it was and run off and find grandfather so that he got instructions where all these loads had to go to.

Then my uncle went to work for them, because they had quite a big transport section developing and he was interested in cars and lorries. There was always a race to the pits in South Yorkshire. They used to hurtle along the road at a great pace because, you see, whoever got to the pits first and got under the supply places first, got the loads and came back first, could have an easier day. There was a great cat and mouse game went on because the police would stand by expecting to catch them speeding.

But when my grandfather retired he got a very tiny pension, and if he had to contact his employer about this he always used to write what he had to say and then he used to put at the bottom, "your humble servant, Fred." We laugh about it now because we got this impression that it was a case of 'touching your forelock,' because a marked respect and a great obedience to your employer was terribly important, otherwise if you said a word out of place or you did your job wrong you'd no redress, and you would be completely without resources and, I suppose in his case, he would have been without a house as well!"

*F. Born 1929*

"My mother was an orphan and an old woman took her in, and this old woman died so they put her in a home. And when she was eight year old she had to go in the mill, and she had to have a buffet to stand on to get up to the looms. A woman looked after them all and they'd to do all their own washing at night, baking bread, everything. Anyway, when I were little she went out charring for eightpence an hour. She worked for a big mill owner in Keighley called Sir Swire Smith. She baked her own bread and Sir Swire Smith used to go crackers on this bread. She used to take him up four or five loaves at a time. Then she worked for Haggas's. Well Sir James Haggas he were a right posh fellow. When he wanted to go to the toilet she couldn't go into the hall to do the cleaning. She had to stop outside till he came back you see. At night she'd be going out helping with these big dinners they had. Sometimes she'd bring a big lump of meat home, they'd sent from the table, and the kitchen staff had had all what they wanted, and then they gave it to my mother. I'll always remember once they sent a big rice pudding, it had never been touched. And if she got anywhere where there were girls like me, they'd send clothes for me to wear. A woman minded us when my mother was charring, and she'd a right big hump on her back, so I used to have to wheel my brother in this bassinet backwards and forwards in the house."

*F. Born 1906*

"A Hattersley loom works with a shuttle, normally a wooden shuttle which is picked across from one side of the loom to the other, and this shuttle carries a yarn package which is of limited size. The machine didn't require a great deal of maintenance and the maintenance didn't need to be terribly skilled, it was more the 'big hammer' rather than the screwdriver. The firm was founded in 1789 by Richard Hattersley who, having completed his

*Croft's Engineering Ltd., Empire Works, Thornbury, 1950.*

apprenticeship at Kirkstall forge, moved to Keighley and set up a forge making nuts and bolts, which later developed into making spindles and flyers for spinning machines, then expanded into making looms, weaving machinery. Before the First World War my grandfather would travel quite extensively in Eastern Europe where we did a lot of trade in those days. Before the Second World War our exporting area was to what was the then British Empire, which would be Australia, New Zealand as our main export market.

I would say the decline set in during the last war (WW2) when the Swiss, who were not involved with the war, had nothing else to do but use their minds to invent new ideas. After the war they came out with some modern machines which were way ahead of ours. Also the Swiss textile machinery firms were mainly parts of big organisations like the Sulzer Corporation, who are reputed to have spent £8,000,000 on their machines before they sold the first one, and spent eight years developing it, and a firm our size could never have withstood that sort of capital expenditure.

Originally it started one loom to one weaver 150 years ago and then two, then four looms to a weaver. A Sulzer loom now would probably be eight, twelve, or sixteen to a weaver, depending on the type of cloth that's woven and the quality required. The speed is also probably four or five times greater than the Hattersley loom.

After WW2 the only new markets would be abroad. Very few people were starting weaving mills in this country. It was more the developing countries, Africa, South Africa, the Middle East. To a certain extent the developing countries weren't ready for the more sophisticated looms. Our type of machine was more suitable for the early days and the name Hattersleys was well known everywhere, having been in business longer than anyone else."

*M. Born 1929*

"Harry worked for Charles Semon's at the end of Bolton Road and he told me, "I don't know how you do it Fred," he says. "Your cloths, you're threepence a yard cheaper than we are," he says, "and you give far more weight than we do and," he says, "your width is always right." He says, "Nobody knows how you do it." And spies from all the manufacturing firms in Bradford used to come when the dyers were delivering. They got to know roughly what time they'd be coming, and you'd see them come and they would be looking at the piece tickets on them. Then the dyers got wise to it, you see. Every wagon that came, all the piece tickets were kept inside."

*M. Born 1910*

"Some of my earliest recollections in the 1920's are of my father working as a cart driver, taking boiler coal to the mills. They did eight journeys a day from City Road Station to Thomas Howarth's Woolcombers in Longside Lane. And then at about five o'clock in the evening they would start and load ashes from the mills to take them to the tips. I remember when I was at Whetley Lane Infants School, during the afternoons when it was quiet, I could hear horses and carts going up Whetley Lane to Lister's Mill with coal. And at the same period Lister's were using steam wagons to take coal, we could always hear the steam wagons go past.

At one period my father worked for Henry North's, Dyers. They were on Plumpton Street in Brownroyd. They were warp dyers. He would do three journeys a week into Lancashire, delivering and collecting undyed warps. He would set off at six o'clock Sunday evening and return to the stables in the early hours of Tuesday morning. Then at nine o'clock they had to be at the stables to do a day's town work. Then once again at six o'clock Tuesday evening they were expected to set off for Lancashire. They saw practically nothing of their families, because the few hours they did spend at home were spent sleeping. Their first stop would usually be at the White Bear at Eastburn. They would feed their horses then yoke up again and continue delivering en route throughout the night. Provision was usually made at different mills for them to leave their warps in some convenient position in the mills without anyone being there. Then they carried on through the day to Colne, Briarfield, Barrowford and on to Burnley."

*F. Born 1922*

"I'd started by cleaning windows at the big houses in Shipley, and things progressed from there. You'd do some paint washing for customers, and then I met this painting and decorating contractor and he invited me to wash some paints for him at a mill where he had a contract. And this was W. J. Whitehead's at Laisterdyke. We washed the ambulance room down, and then he gave us small painting jobs at different mills, and eventually I took it up myself. I got a partner and we went into painting and decorating. We got the contract for all the window cleaning at Whitehead's, and then we started doing the painting work there. And the first job we did was a big spinning room. I'd never done a big job like that in my life before. I'd got it on price and I'd to make it pay, and I'd no

*Some large firms had their own interests outside the mill. For example Lister's had their own colleries in Wales, and railway rolling stock to transport the coal.*

idea about ordering quantities of paint for big jobs. But we did the job, we made a profit, and Mr Booth, the chief engineer at Whiteheads at that time, he was delighted with the job. I'd taken old sheets from home to cover the machines because it was not like today when you can cover everything with polythene. Originally it was all lime washing. All the mills used to be limed out during the annual closedown. A terrible job it was, if you got any lime in your eyes you really suffered. Eventually I think we did every room there is at Whitehead's. Those that work there work in one room and they go home, but you, as a contractor, often get into every nook and cranny so you know more about that mill than those who work there. I remember when we started, seeing sixty or seventy woolsorters on one floor. You go back today and you've got five in that room, and they are simply putting wool down different holes because it virtually comes sorted today. Where there were maybe twenty, thirty carding machines, six or seven will do the work now because they're big and they produce more, it is fantastic. I've worked in most of the mills in and around Bradford over the years but the one I'm proud of is Jerome's of Shipley, to go back as a contractor having worked there as a bobbin-ligger you know. I've lost a tremendous amount of contracts over the last few years because of mills being closed, amalgamations and then being demolished. The newer machines have produced more with less operatives, less space needed, so therefore, you close down."

*M. Born 1927*

*Traders on the floor of the Wool Exchange, 1904.*

# THE TRADE

"To know what was happening … you went into the Wool Exchange"

"When I first started in 1923 the only sort of touch many of us had with the outside world, to know what was happening in say Sydney, was in the Wool Exchange. It was just spinners downwards, generally speaking, was the Wool Exchange. Pure manufacturers or piece merchants or piece dyers or that sort of thing didn't come in there.

The cables would be pinned to the notice board, you know, from sales in Australia or change of bank rate or anything. The spinners and top-makers were there. Quotes would be given to the spinner and then his competitor, and by a sort of 'bush telegraph' it would soon get around, and that's how the price was set. These were for wool textiles throughout the whole world, a really important thing. I had a friend who was a national correspondent for Reuters and those prices were then sent all over the world.

I myself have sold millions of pounds worth of things on word of mouth. The honour amongst the trade was fantastic. The wool textile industry throughout the world was a very large family really.

A tremendous lot of business was done in the clubs and cafes around the Wool Exchange. Most of the manufacturers had offices in Swan Arcade, Charles Street, Booth Street, you know. So people would filter into Bradford around ten-ish when they'd done their mail. There was the Central Cafe, the Mecca, Collinson's, the Exchange, the Cuba, all these cafes where businessmen, wool men, waste men, noil men, carriers, railwaymen, all sorts of people met, and the great thing they did was play dominoes. Some, of course, went to the Union Club in Piece Hall. The German merchants were very instrumental in forming that particular Club. We'd five main gentlemen's clubs — there was the Conservative Club, the Liberal Club, the Bradford Club and the Union Club."

*M. Born 1901*

"I remember once going down Silsden main street, and a manufacturer shouted across the street to me. "Oh Tom," he said "We want some more looms." "Oh," I said, "How many Mr Hill?" He said, "Sixty." "Half right and half left?" "Yes, just like the last lot." "Right," I said, "We'll confirm it." And that was an order for sixty looms. Shouted across the street! There was a lot of that done then."

*M. Born 1901*

"In 1931, a slump, everybody in the firm got a reduction, 10 shillings here, five bob there, everybody except me. He couldn't do it to me because I had a contract. So I went to him, "Mr Selka, I understand everybody in the firm has had a reduction except me. I know I have an agreement but I would like to be in the same position as everybody else." He says, "Right, drop £2 a week!" "Confound me," says I, "I should have kept me mouth shut!""

*M. Born 1903*

"I was once coming out of Benn's at Beckside, Clayton, with Harry Wood, who was a proper Bradford wool man. And there was a great wagon stood outside with South American bales of wool. Harry pulled a bit out, felt at it and said, "Good Lord, they're all wringing wet are these bales. It's very serious. What we've got to find out is whether they're fresh-water damaged or sea-water damaged because the claim will have to be either against the shipping people or the transport people." So he took a piece and tasted it. "Oh God — Ooh" he said, "It's salt water, ugh, terrible." So he went back to the office, and as he got there the telephone went, "Ah this is so-and-so at Liverpool. Have you any wool off such-and-such a ship?" "Yes, yes we have." They said, "Well on no account must anybody touch it," they said "it's been stored on the ship next to some hides which are infected with anthrax." And old Harry's on the phone, he went green as grass! "Touch it," he said, "I've just **eaten** some." Still nothing happened, but there it was."

*M. Born 1901*

"I joined the old Shipley branch of the Woolsorters' Society. The only time I can remember a dispute situation was over some Irish wool. Often the problems were the pricing for a job, and they gave a price for this job and we couldn't make money at it. It was full of grass, straw, you name it, it was in, and we just couldn't make money at it. So we got management up and we discussed it and they said, "Well, I'm sorry, but for the price on the job we're receiving we can't afford to give you any more." "Well we can't afford to sort it for that price." "Well if you can't afford to sort it for that price, we'll have to send it out on commission." "So do that," we said, "but we're certainly not sorting it at that price." And whatever happened to it I don't know, we never saw the wool, but there's nobody could have made money at the prices they wanted to pay."

*M. Born 1946*

"You weren't allowed to be in a trade union. We certainly weren't in unions, in the clerical side of the textiles. We were right in between the union people and the bosses, and you just attended and did your work, and worked Saturdays to keep your money going and hoped you got a rise at Christmas. The interesting thing is, you see, the different approach to us in those days. I remember when I went down to the wool exhibition in the Midland in Forster Square, and I attended because I was interested in textile fibres. But when I attended the hotel they asked me where I came from, and I was only a young man at the time, and I said I was from Courtauld's, and he said, "Well, you can ruddy well get out of here," he says, "that's synthetic rubbish." And that really upset me in a way, because I thought we were all working together. It was my first indication, that not all wool people, or even textile people, work together."

*M. Born 1924*

*Wool warehousing along Canal Road, c.1900.*

"With the nylon, you see, they hadn't found a way then of removing oil marks, and you had to keep dipping your hands in French chalk so that you didn't put finger marks on. And if the sun was shining through the roof and the rays were going onto the machine where you were winding nylon, you had to cover it up with brown paper to keep the sun off, because it used to turn the nylon yellow, and they wanted it white."

*M. Born 1910*

"It was April forty-nine when I went to Fisher's, and I were there while 1952 when it was National Service. And all that time I went to evening classes at Bradford Tech. But the machines in Fishers were all built at Keighley, and they were all Prince Smiths machines and Stells, and all the bobbins etc were all made at just past Keighley, at Steeton.

Fisher's Mill was really old, it was prosperous in them days, but the problem with it was that all the machinery was Prince Smith and Stell's, and it all used to come in on the railway you see. It's like Whitehead's, they had their own sidings on the railways to run the machines from Keighley where they made the machines, through, and the same applied to Idle.

The machines came into Idle station and then they went down on carts, rollers, into Fishers. All the machines were made of the best steel, you see. Now that was the problem with Prince Smiths. Prince Smiths built a machine that had to last for fifty-odd years or even hundred years, so there was never any follow up. Prince Smith's sold you a gill-box, which is a drawing machine, and that gill-box had to last probably the lifetime of the mill owner and into his next generation. And they were made so well, machined so well out of the best steel, with great big roller-bearing brasses which apprentices and oilers had to keep oiled, that they were virtually everlasting. In fact you could get one of those old gill-boxes now which are in the museum and run it, and it would run perfectly. The difference was that you used to produce something like two hundred and fifty pounds a week out of a gill-box. There was never any shift work, shift work was never a concept. There were never no night shift. There might have been a bit of evening shift when the mill had an excess of orders, or it had an order to get out, then they would work an evening shift, but it would be the same workers that worked that day. Now we used to go down at seven till about five. Seven, half past seven, quarter to eight, as progressively working week dropped. I think when I started, the guaranteed working week was forty seven and half, and it's gradually come down, but there were never no evening shift.

But the machines that were scrapped out of Fishers were just as good as when they were put in. The only difference was that other people had modernised, and therefore what is today a gill box will do a thousand kilos a shift. We used to do two hundred and fifty pounds a week."

*M. Born 1934*

"After the war finished in forty-five we were re-equipping with machinery. In those days it was mostly made in the U.K., a lot of it in Keighley at Prince, Smith and Stell's and Hattersleys and so forth, and we were re-equipping with looms, and Noble combs. I think it's fair to say we didn't make vast profits, and it turned the tide and we could then re-invest. The Korean War gave a tremendous boost to textiles. Everybody was very nervous there was going to be another world war and the price of raw materials rocketed to an all time high, but then of course came down to all time low. That was a very big turning point in the fortunes, I think, of the wool textile industry. But between the end of the war and the Korean war everybody was busy building up and replacing what had gone, and the Korean war accentuated this, and then, of course, once that was resolved to some degree, the raw material price sank like a stone, very rapidly, and a lot of people went bust."

*M. Born 1924*

"In the late forties through to the mid-fifties one fabric which was paramount in a lot of mills in Bradford was Union gabardine, worsted warp, cotton weft, piece-dyed. And there was an attitude that, as Union gabardine is here to stay, it will never disappear, and it disappeared in about 18 months, never to be seen again, virtually. There's never such a thing as 'it will never stop' or 'it will always be' in textiles. It just doesn't happen that way. Unfortunately the change that everyone acknowledges will happen, happens so quickly that they've been unable to adapt to the fresh one, and by the time they have they've lost business, and if you lose business at that rapidity certain mills must go with it."

*M. Born 1929*

*Stencilling destinations on finished products.*

"Twenty, thirty years ago there were four hundred sorters, now there's forty. They used to do four bales a day each, now they do forty. There's not the sorting there used to be. Instead of it being sorted into many different qualities, nowadays the wool is being graded in where it has come from, whereas the wool would be more mixed in the bale before. The only job when they do any sorting is English wool. It's a lot different sort of wool, and they need to look at it more, pick grey out and grit, things like that. A lot of sorters went out of the trade. Thirty years ago you could get jobs at Baird's, or making tractors, but nowadays you can't. In fact they have a big list now down at the Sorters' Club waiting for jobs. Even last year where I worked there was another dozen made redundant. It is a dying job really."

*M. Born 1944*

*Directors of a Bradford spinning mill, 1930s.*

"Before the war (WW2) they went in for quality, not quantity. A lot used to go to America. They would pay the earth for a wool and mohair suit. And also I think the owners loved a good reputation, that was precious to them, an award for fine quality yarn, it was important to them. But then came a slack period, like there is after every war. Every time a war starts the money comes out of the walls, out of the woodwork, it does really! But when the war is over then the money goes away, and we were on three days a week for a long time. It was a very slack period for nearly two years. Then when trade did pick up again it was spasmodic. For about five or six years you'd be busy, you'd be slack, you'd be busy, you'd be slack, and then gradually it built up and it was quite steady again until about 1976 when all these factories started becoming redundant. That was really tragic because of the skilled people who worked in there, it was heartbreaking. There were whole families, you could have as many as five or six

*Modernised spinning mill. Those mills which survive today have invested in automated machinery which can produce vast quantities of the product at great speed, with a much reduced workforce.*

people from one family all working in the mill, and all of a sudden the bottom fell out of their little world and there was no work."

*F. Born 1924*

"In the seventies with Ted Heath and all the screaming, everybody else worked a three day week, **we** worked seven days. Simple, we've got a steam engine which gave us enough horse power to keep going. We used the National Grid for the three days working week and then we ran the rest of the week on the steam engine. We were working overtime."

*M. Born 1934*

"The old machines we've been taking out have gone overseas. Because of cheap labour they can still be competitive. I've seen weaving sheds in India, on T.V.,

*Manningham Mills, 1989. These empty buildings are to be converted into a branch of The Victoria and Albert Museum.*

exactly like Bradford, all the old Hattersley looms bashing away."

*M. Born 1933*

"Then they stuck us on what they call three days a week, that is, you work three days and you sign on three days and that went on for quite a while. Then it got you'd work two days and sign on four days, and eventually there was no work at all."

*M. Born 1939*

"And when I first began working I thought Bradford and its wool trade would go on for ever. My daughter, she's at college doing a course on computers, so when she leaves with her computer training, if she does go into textiles I think there'll be more future for her then, than in other respects. I think she's in the industry of today."

*F. Born 1939*

*Asian, Polish and English workmates at A. P. Taylor's, Shipley, 1964.*

# IMPORTED LABOUR

"Don't wait for any posh jobs"

"When we first arrived in Bradford, top of Leeds Road, it was a very, very hot day. I can remember the stench of unwashed wool was so strong it was overpowering. And I said to the others "I just don't know how people can live in a place with that stench lingering in the town."

*F. Born 1931*

"At Drummond's in the early thirties the principal operatives were Bradford people, but eventually these people said, "Listen we're not working for this, we can get better jobs in Woolworths or the market. To hell with textiles." So then we had Irish girls coming. A local woman would put them up, say, three in a little bedroom. We brought some from Barnsley and places like that. A lot of manufacturers brought girls from the mining areas. Then soon after the war a lot of Poles came here. They'd come from textile places in Poland and we employed quite a lot of them because they were very good workers, and they showed some of our British workpeople up, particularly when it was piece work, like burling and mending. They could do a piece in half the time that English girls could do it. Anyway from then we started getting Pakistanis, mostly male, very few women. You see today the machinery has been hotted up much more than when it was manual. With all this automation you don't need a girl. The only place you need them is the burling and mending, which is really a needlework job."

*M. Born 1903*

"Anyway, when it came to choose the country, we choose England. We set off from Germany in May 1947, and we came to England in June 1947. We were placed in Full Sutton camp near York. All we wanted is to be settled, to find a place where we're going to live, and then we were taken to work. They came one day and selected several families. There were about six families, about three families Ukrainian, Estonian and Latvian, and they put us in a bus and brought us to Bradford. Actually we were the first Ukrainian families that came to Bradford, and we were placed in a hostel in Shearbridge Road. There was a burling and mending place underneath and on the first floor there was a big corridor which was divided in little partitions, and these little partitions, like little rooms, were given for each family. They were all married families. We had one ceiling just divided half way, across the rooms. And we were working in Peel Brothers, City Road. And so when they brought us to this factory, they showed us all the departments where we can work, and there was a big hall where all ladies sat there doing the mending. And so I came to work among English ladies."

*F. Born 1923*

"The Government was bringing them into Bradford to supplement the labour forces in the Mills, and also because they had to do something with them. So we were receiving batches of what they called European Voluntary Workers, and they arrived with more or less the clothes that they stood up in. I mean they'd nothing, and they had to be housed and trained and put into the mills. Now the object of the exercise, I know it's all wrong now, but the object of the exercise then was called Integration. It was the policy of the Government to integrate these people into our society and that was, from the word go, the policy they adopted. I mean I went round Bradford on my own, into all sorts of houses looking for accommodation. We advertised and people answered the adverts and we'd say, "Have you got a spare room?"

We had to negotiate all this with the Labour Exchange. They used to bring them over to places like Full Sutton in England, and then you'd go over and interview a few. The employers would send representatives and interview a few, and then your batch would arrive at a pre-arranged time, and, I mean, you didn't know when they were going to come. We used to have a contract with a taxi firm and they'd bring them to the mill, and then we'd take them out in these taxis to all these landladies and they would put them up in their accommodation. You got people who were called Link Couples, a man and woman who had started to live together as man and wife, but who weren't really married because they perhaps didn't know whether their husband or wife had been killed or, you know, they just didn't know where they were. And we used to put them in as married couples, but we didn't take many married couples simply because there weren't many jobs in textiles for men. We liked girls if we could get them.

Health wise they were well, and they were very hard workers. They very quickly learned. I mean, they only learned because you put them with other people, and they very quickly learned the job and they saved money. There was a lot of feeling among the workers. I mean, they used to say, "Huh, we might as well raise the Red Flag here if we're going to bring any more of these folk here," and, you know, "The place is full of foreigners," and that sort of thing.

I don't remember people asking them about their experiences because our whole attitude was to get them settled into the mill. They wanted to be earning money, they wanted to get some kind of dignity back, I suppose. They didn't want to give any sort of offence, because if they gave offence, not only would they lose their job, they'd be deported. In fact, we did have one girl who was deported. They were deported back to Europe, which was the last thing they wanted, because many of them knew if they went back to Europe either the Russians or the Germans would put them to death. So it wasn't a subject that you talked about.

I stayed thirteen years at Briggella Mills and some of them were still there. I mean, they'd got a job and they'd got settled and they didn't move. When they first came they were under strict supervision, they had work permits, and they had to register with the Police. They had to have permission to move their job and they could only move their job if the Ministry of Labour knew where they were going. So they were very heavily supervised. That restriction lasted for about three or four years, I think, and then it was lifted and they were allowed to move about in society just like ordinary English people were. But by then they'd saved every penny that they could earn. They ate very frugally, really frugally, very simple, frugal meals. When they bought clothes they bought one good suit. The women all went and bought black costumes with white blouses. That's probably what they wore in their own country, and you'd see them all walking up and down town with these black costumes on, really good material. But they had that and their working clothes, and then every other penny went into the Bank, and as soon as ever they could they were buying houses, trying to establish themselves one way or another, and, of course, as soon as they were able they left. I mean particularly the men left the mills, and the women of course, if their husbands got good jobs.

I think they were relieved about coming here. They were at least into a situation where they had a job and they could earn money, and there was eventually hope of getting some control over their own lives, and freedom from fear really. And after the E.V.W.'s came that solved our labour problem for the time, but then when they began to assimilate or integrate into the community we were still left with a labour problem, and we began to bring Italians across and we bought hostels for them, and we'd bought a hostel out at Longlands."

*F. Born 1929*

"We, as English people, were content to work five days a week all the year round, but some of the foreign workers would work Saturday, Sunday and they'd add another day and hope the Lord wouldn't see it. The Eastern Europeans would work every hour that God sends, and we weren't prepared to do that. We were content with a steady income every week, so we found then that things did change quite a lot. But I learned a lot of Italians how to do the knots and how to work the machines. I worked mainly with Italians and one or two Polish people. They were very good hard working people. But with the piece work the antagonism started to creep in. We found that the bosses preferred to employ these people who were willing to work dreadfully long hours. The Unions had got us down to working a forty hour week, you see what I mean, and they were willing to work over Saturday and Sunday, and we didn't think that was right because Sunday was the Lord's day. We worked Sundays when the war was on, but there was a need for it. We did it for the war effort more or less. But then we expected it to stop, you see. And then the other thing came in, day turn, evening shift (which was unheard of), and then all night. It was good from the point of view that it provided more people with jobs, but on the other hand one machine like the Schlaflorst automatic winder running day, evening and night replaced about forty women."

*F. Born 1924*

"We came from Pordenone to Milan, sixteen of us from the North, and then we met a group of girls from the South, and all together we were about eighty, but we came accompanied with an interpreter and nurse from England, on the train. They came to pick us up when we arrived at Victoria Station. I expected something beautiful, but at the time it was very, **very** dirty and everything seemed to be so **black.** We were very distressed, **very** distressed. But then we got to the King's Cross to come to Bradford, it was dark and we arrived in Bradford at half-past-eleven in the evening, so we couldn't see anything. We only saw that it was very dark, houses, everything was dark! Raining, awful, oh, **terrible** weather it was. But the shock we got when we went to the hostel in Queensbury, we didn't see nothing at night, we were absolutely tired, and we all gone to bed, five in room for a start, but that wasn't too bad. You know, we didn't want to stay, and then the interpreter came and she says to be ready for eleven o'clock to go and visit the factory. So we did. Once we visit the factory it didn't seem too bad, but too noisy, very **noisy.** But, when I look around, I said "Oh there is one particular place that I would like to work," because they were very good, we had a choice to pick the job we wanted. They show us all the jobs in the factory and they ask us which jobs we would prefer. So I says "I wouldn't mind doing burling and mending," because I see the ladies all sitting down and doing something with material. So I says "Put my name down for burling and mending," which I wasn't lucky to get straight away. We had to go to work for three months in fly-spinning. That was an experience, it was **absolutely impossible.** But anyway, after a week we just got going and then we seemed to get used to the idea, but still I wanted to do burling and mending, because I felt that it was the best job for me."

*F. Born 1931*

"They brought some Italian girls, about thirty, forty years since. And they brought these girls in, and we were on the old machinery then. They brought them just before Christmas. They brought four perhaps into our room. They spread them round the room. And they couldn't speak a word of English, this were the trouble, and you had to teach them how to do the job. Well it was most difficult because they'd never seen anything like it before, and they'd come straight from home. These Italian girls that we got they'd never worked, they'd always been at home, sewing, you see, they were very good at sewing and needlework, but they'd never worked outside in a mill or factory or anything, and it were all so new to them. Well I couldn't speak Italian, so you'd to do it by sign language you see, you'd to say ... "One, two, three, four." We gradually got them learned, but it were a very difficult job. It were hard work, because you had to be watching all the time. I had one Italian girl and she were forever putting her fingers into the wheel, you know, and I'd to smack her hands for her. I said "I'll smack your hands if you don't give up." Now the first lot they brought, they came just about a month before Christmas. Well it were **pathetic,** because they were away from home and their parents and everything at Christmas. And we'd bought them a Christmas present, and of course buying them this Christmas present upset them because they knew we were trying to be friends with them and they were so far away from home. One Italian girl, I had her for Christmas and then we took her out one night to the theatre to see the 'La Boheme' you know, things like that. Now the overlooker we had, he could speak a bit of Italian and he could talk to them you see, and explain what we were trying to do, but you see you couldn't be with one particular person **all** the time so it were, it were very difficult when they came."

*F. Born 1921*

"I can't remember ever having any European Immigrants

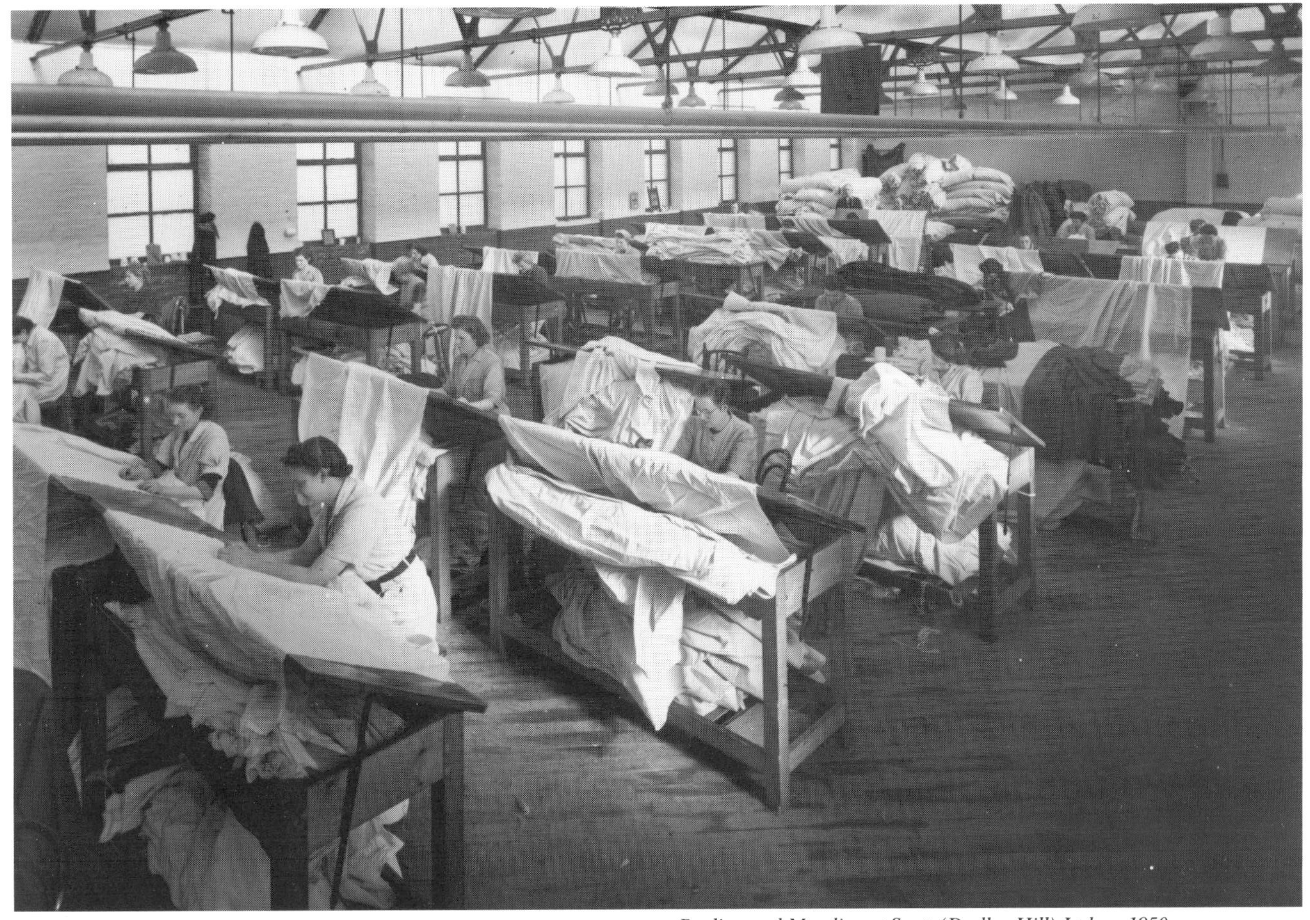

*Burling and Mending at Scott (Dudley Hill) Ltd., c.1950.*

in the dyehouse. You see we operated a closed shop. We had girls working at Salt's in the spinning and weaving, things like that, you know from Italy and places like that. They built a special hostel for them in the works itself. They took a section of the mill over and fitted it up with bedroom suites and all like that."

*M. Born 1910*

"Young people didn't want to come to woolcombing. It was a dirty job, smelly job, you know, when water's boiling and you were washing raw wool in that, so you can imagine how pleasant a smell it was. And especially when we used to get human hair from Korea, you know, during Korean war, and it was filthy that hair. Some people were off for three or four weeks poorly with that smell."

*M. Born 1923*

"The problem of communication is this, that the Polish people here, with few exceptions, didn't see any need in learning the English language in the very beginning. Maybe they didn't have the opportunity, because if you work in textiles, and dust and noisy conditions, who do you talk to? To nobody! You know, you talk to yourself, and then when you come home to your Polish wife or to your Polish husband for that matter, then you converse in the language which is the easiest. Then I think it is also true that some Poles lived with the hope that one day sooner or later the Polish question would be resolved and everybody was going to return, so what's the point? But then you talk to Poles who knew that whatever happens, "I'm here, be it for a short time or long time, I have to master the language." But unfortunately lack of communication is something which breeds isolation, and so forth, and from here you can go on and on and on, and then you can see how the problems will mount. Because if you feel threatened, if you feel not wanted, if you can't communicate with the indigenous population, then obviously you become more and more insular. You lose the will to be, and then you drift into your past."

*M. Born 1942*

"If you can go back to nineteen fifties, there was a boom, especially in the textiles, and they couldn't find enough people to run the mills, so getting jobs were no problem, you know. I even remember, when I came across to England, they still had the big boards outside the big old factories saying "Vacancies." And all you had to do was just walk down the street and say "Oh yes, there's a job there," and you'd go in and you'd get a job. So getting jobs in them days was no problem. You could actually pick and choose. You worked there one week and say, "Oh no, I'll go to another one." So there was no problem in that, and the jobs were mainly semi-skilled, labour work, you didn't need to be able to read and write really, or even speak, you know. The task was so simple."

*M. Born 1953*

"My friend's younger brother, he says, "Don't wait for any posh jobs. All Indian and Pakistanis, they work in factories here, so you've got to work in a factory. You've got to accept this, right? Don't wait for any special jobs. If somebody's telling you that because you were a solicitor and you had degrees and all that, and you will get any special job, then forget about it." So after two days he told me that this is the rule, this is the rule. Just keeping on working, the factories, and factories and factories."

*M. Born 1938*

"When I joined the company in 1959 one of the first things that I was able to recommend was the running of a night shift. English people didn't want to work at night due to the unsocial hours aspect of it, but we then had a large immigrant population coming in who were quite happy to work at night. The case that I put was that if we trained one or two as a nucleus and were confident that they knew the job, we could then bring in numbers and gradually we could use them to train their own countrymen. That worked very well and we started to run at night in 1961. We explained the move to Pakistani and Indian labour to the rest of the workforce to pre-empt any difficulties in that direction by saying that it was essential for survival for us to run three shifts and they would be on from nine o'clock at night to eight o'clock in the morning. And by explaining it to small groups of people we got this point of view across and we never had the slightest resistance to them coming in."

*M. Born 1936*

"My cousin had just arrived from England, he was boasting about his life, about his job in England, and what a wonderful time he had in England, what a load of money he earned, and he was talking about his mill. He had brought lots of presents for his wife and for his kids, and he was wearing this very expensive suit, and I got very envious, because I was only earning about thirty rupees a month in the Army. My cousin was saying, "When I get to work there's a machine there with two buttons, a red one

*Highly automated machinery was very efficient, but labour was needed to run it 24 hours a day to make a return on the investment. Winding department, 1970.*

and a green one, and if I press the green one the machine starts, you press the red one the machine stops, and that's my work. And then I go home and I earn tons of money for doing that. The houses are big, you know, you have a wonderful life there." So I decided to apply, I resigned from the Army and I applied to come to England. I went to Karachi, and at that time they used to have agents that used to set up your ticket and everything, and you had to have a sponsor in England. And my younger brother actually was in England working in a Dewsbury mill, and he sponsored me. And I had to raise six thousand rupees for my passage over. So my brother sent me some money and I paid this money to the agents and I came to England in 1961.

I was very happy. I thought to myself I was going to a country, a rich country, and I was going to earn a lot of money and would have a good living, and I was just excited about coming over to England. But at that time things, the job situation was pretty bad, and I asked my brother to find me a job, and he enquired at his place of work for a job for me. Eventually he found me a job. It was weaving, nights, it was a very hard job, all night you had to stand. Difficult, a very hard job. But slowly I began to pick it up and I got used to it, and the money was okay.

The management at that time was very good towards us because we, the Asian workers were very, very hard-working. But we felt that we did receive some sort of resentment from the other English workers, the reason for that being because as far as they were concerned we caused a bit of a problem for them, because we worked extra hard and faster than they did. And wherever, whichever department an Asian worker went you'd find that English workers slowly moved out of there. I think we were all aware of our obligations, that's why we had to work that much harder, and that much longer, in order to earn enough money to send back to Pakistan as well as for our upkeep in this country."

*M. Born 1932*

"And then we started getting one or two Asians, and some of the spinners that came as jobbers in the sixties are still with us. I've got an Arab who came jobber-ladding at that time — he's now overlooking. I've got three Jamaicans — and they've been with me now for about six years. One came from Croft's when they shut the foundry down. He came to me one night when I was on nights and said "I can't get a job anywhere." I said "Well come on, I'll give you a chance," and I put him in the drawing. He probably took a 50% reduction coming to work in textiles from engineering, but he stuck with it and I admire him for it. At one time you got something like 90% immigrants on nights at Whitehead's. Now you've got 2nd generation immigrants with Yorkshire accents, and I have a lass who says "Why aye man," so she obviously comes from Durham."

*M. Born 1934*

*J. H. Binns and Co., trip to Blackpool, 1919.*

# SOCIAL LIFE

"I joined Lister's boxing club and I won a carving knife"

"We used to sit on the top of our outside toilet in Picton Street and look to the bottom of the street over into Peel Park when the Gala was on. All the children used to accumulate on our lavatory top and we'd sit there with a bag of chips and watch the firework display. This was the highlight of the year. Neighbours used to bring us a cup of tea or pop and we were allowed to stay up till about half-past nine. I miss the old 'tides,' the fairgrounds with the big steam boats, Shamrock and Columbia and the Cakewalk."

*M. Born 1921*

"Whit Monday and we'd set off all behind one another, you know, and there'd be the choir master, they called him Harold Church and we'd stop at somebody's house perhaps, somebody that were getting old, and then we'd stand there and sing. And he used to have a pitch-fork and I can remember him tapping this pitch-fork on the wall and he'd go, "Doh, ray, me, fah, soh, lah, tee," (laughter), and then we had to start to sing, and there were some lovely hymns sung on these Whit Mondays. Perhaps walking round the village at the same time there'd be the Parish Church going round as well, but they were always fortunate, you see, because the Foster family, being in with the Parish Church, they always had the Black Dyke band leading their procession. So if ever we could get to a house where the Black Dyke Band were playing, say in the next street, we sang the hymn Black Dyke Band were playing, so that we had the Black Dyke Band accompanying us. And then, if it were a fine day we'd go down into a field belonging to an old farmer called Willie Binns, that were on Deanstones Lane, Blackmires Farm it were called, and we used to have what we called a long bun, as dry as old sticks, and a pot of tea, and then they'd run races and play games and that was your Whit Monday."

*F. Born 1921*

"There was a Girls' Club attached to Black Dyke that Miss Gwen Foster, Mr Edward Anderton Foster's daughter, ran in the Victoria Hall. And once they took us to York to see the Five Sisters Windows, and then we would have an ordinary social, you know. I would sing and somebody else would recite and that, and I remember very vividly a Miss Louthward coming to talk to us, and she came from a Home for Fallen Girls on Manningham Lane. And I remember the words she finished with, she said "There is nothing in this world like a good woman," so I've always remembered that."

*F. Born 1908*

"On the occasions that my father did go out for a drink it would be the holiday period. Maybe he'd meet his brothers, because he was one of seven brothers, and they would meet occasionally, but the money they had to spare was so limited, they couldn't, you know, drink to that extent, and it was very rare that they bought each other drinks like they do today. But everybody respected that because they were in the same boat; they would have a glass as against a pint of beer, but they would get the companionship of dominoes and darts and all the rest of it."

*F. Born 1924*

"There used to be the Children's Treats from Sunday School, and invariably for an occasion like that the cart horses were decorated, and it was normal custom to decorate a horse for May Day. Some of the horses were entered for local shows. There were classes for the 'cleanest horses and harness' and it was a matter of pride for a driver to win one of those classes."

*M. Born 1922*

"You'd got to go to the Baptist Chapel to get a job at Smith's (Allerton) and if you wanted to go to the Allerton Combing Company you had to go to the Congregational Chapel, and if you wanted to work for Wood's you'd got to go to the Wesleyans."

*M. Born 1915*

*Husband and Wife at a Mill Party, 1950s.*

"From the top of Queensbury to the top of Mill Lane, just that small stretch used to be what they called the "Prom," and on a Sunday night you used to walk up and down. I met one or two of my boyfriends that way. There weren't many boys in the weaving, but in the spinning or twisting there were boys and young men that were overlookers and that's how you met them, and going to the pictures and sitting in the back row, and such as that."

*F. Born 1908*

"When I met my husband I worked at Cawthra's at the time, and they'd a lovely canteen and they used to have dances there every Saturday night. My father was very, very strict but he always let me go to these dances at the mill because he knew where I was. It was New Year's Eve, 1925. I was 17 and me and my mate were dancing together, and for some reason she got a bit upset and just walked off and left me, and this boy must have seen this and he came straight up to me. And he turned out to be the brother of Doris who I worked with, and that's how I met him. Ah, and he had a motorbike and he used to come and meet me from work because he worked at the B.D.A. and it was notorious for short time work was the B.D.A. And he used to come on the days he wasn't working, and he'd be waiting at Cawthra's mill gates with his motorbike. And in those days you didn't sit cock-stride, you sat side-saddle, and when my mother saw me sat on the pillion, side-saddle, she nearly died!"

*F. Born 1908*

"I signed on for Manningham Mills Juniors. I played with them two or three seasons and then I left them and went to Salem Athletic. I were playing 'til I were about twenty-two but I don't think there was a week passed that I didn't come home limping. One week I fell and hurt my shoulder. I had my arm in a sling for a fortnight. Then another time I banged my shoulder and when I got off the field I couldn't undress, the chaps had to help me. They had an insurance scheme and then they'd 'sick money,' but it wasn't as much as what it was when you were working. That's why I couldn't have much time off. But when I were a lad I joined Lister's boxing club and I won a carving knife and a thing to sharpen it on. It were in a long case.

Then I wanted to go see a cup semi-final at Leeds at Elland Road so I pawned it. I took it to a pawn shop in Denby Street at the bottom of Whetley Mill. I got half-a-crown for it and I never bothered redeeming it."

*M. Born 1913*

"C. F. Taylor's, Salt's, Mason's and Shay Mills they all had their football teams, their cricket teams and their boxing teams, particularly the boxing teams because they were during the winter mostly, and you used to go to each venue to watch your mates box. Salt's boxed at the Royal Cafe down Victoria Road. Mason's boxed down in their canteen area and C. F. Taylor's, they had a place down at Baildon Bridge. Lord Barmby was instrumental in starting all this you know. It was a bit different when I worked for the B.D.A., there we used to have interworks teams and the work force on the shop floor used to play the management and office staff."

*M. Born 1910*

"Dudley Ackroyd, a big wool man, Tops and Noils, he used to run Salem Football Club. He wouldn't allow gambling, so what we used to do to raise funds was have a jumble sale and he used to provide about three of his old suits, which were practically brand new, he was a millionaire, and these used to pay for the season's football."

*M. Born 1921*

"At Christmas we'd take some sherry and mince pies and happen a Christmas cake and have a break for about an hour in the afternoon. The weavers, you could hear them going mad, but we weren't with them, we just sat round our mending tables and had us own bit of fun. We never went in any other part of the mill at all."

*F. Born 1915*

"When I worked at Wool Control, the cleaners all used to put tuppence a week away, which meant a lot to me then, and we'd go on the train to Harrogate about twice a year for a meal. It was a right highlight was this meal, although we only ever had sandwiches and a trifle, but you never got trifle at home, never, we didn't anyway!"

*F. Born 1913*

"I did three years at night school, three nights a week, straight from work. And when the Gaumont cinema opened, the first night it opened there was Lister and other chaps, Gerald Whitaker and myself going to night school and we walked past this glittering building, opening night, oh, dear! We got up as far as the Empire, couldn't resist temptation any longer so we went back and

*Team photograph taken at the rear of Lister's Mill, c.1918.*

went in. Up in the balcony, it was either a shilling or one-and-three. Oh, it was magnificent! Three hours and a quarter show! We were late home that night."

*M. Born 1910*

"When I first started work in the mill during the war (WW2) I think the wage where I was, in the drawing, was twenty seven shilling. Well I always tipped up and I only used to get half-a-crown spending money. So what we used to rely on was the bonus. If we'd had a good week we'd take two bob out each for a Thursday night at the 'Ideal,' that was the dance hall at Bankfoot. Half-past-four, when we'd nearly finished we used to wash our legs in the basin and put this leg make-up on, and then one of the lasses would draw a line down the back of your legs with mascara chalk so that it looked like the seam of your stockings. We used to borrow pipe cleaners from each other to curl our hair and swap jigger coats for the night. You see there wasn't many clothes about and they were on coupons. If we'd no money we could play games and music and dancing at the Y.M.C.A. It were only a penny for a cup of tea and you'd the night there. And if we were well off we'd go to the Brown Derby cafe and get beans on toast and a cup of tea for sixpence. Ooh, we were posh!"

*F. Born 1927*

"I remember after the war (WW2) they decided that they'd start another football club and I remember us all going up who were interested and doing the field ourselves, picking all the stones up and cutting the grass and such like. I don't remember getting any help at all from the management, none whatsoever. We did it all ourselves. Then Willie Bennett, this old chap I used to work with, he took a keen interest. He was secretary for this, that and the other, and he used to put lunch-time concerts on. Anybody that worked there that fancied they could sing or whatever used to be doing their stuff on stage. By this time they had a proper sort of theatre and canteen."

*M. Born 1921*

# TEXTILE PROCESSES

During this century the textile centres of West Yorkshire have been able to make a wide range of different qualities and types of cloth, each town specialising in a specific kind of cloth. The Bradford area is famous for the production of worsted cloth, the wool being 'combed' as opposed to 'carded' as in the preparation of woollen cloth. Woollen yarns are made from new wool and recycled wool including noils, and their fibres are not parallel but crossed in all directions giving a rough and whiskery appearance to the spun thread.

The term worsted is used to describe yarns — the material from which woven and knitted fabrics are made — produced from the raw wool only, which has had the short fibres removed by combing and the long fibres laid parallel to produce a smooth, even yarn.

The term 'Worsted' is said to derive from 'Worstead' the name of a village in east Norfolk and meant at first a particular kind of fabric made in that area, but was later used to describe all material manufactured from wholly or partly combed wool.

**SEQUENCE OF PROCESSES**

Sorting: A highly skilled process by which the wool fleece and skin wool is divided manually into defined qualities.

Blending: Wools of similar qualities but different types are blended together to obtain some desired effect or characteristic and to produce a bulk lot for combing.

Scouring: The wool is washed to remove dirt, natural grease, and any other impurities. It is then dried.

Carding: Where the wool fibres are disentangled, vegetable impurities removed, and made into a twistless rope-like form called a sliver.

Preparing: A process used in place of carding for long wools and hairs which would break on the card and therefore greatly reduce the quality of the worsted yarn produced.

Back Washing: A light washing process given to the slivers to remove dirt picked up in carding. The wool is then dried and treated in a gill box to start laying the fibres parallel.

Combing: This is the basic process in the manufacture of worsted yarns and fabrics.

The objects or aims of combing are the straightening of the wool fibres and the separation of the short wool from the long. The short fibres referred to as "noils" are discarded and only the long fibres in the form of a "top" are allowed to go forward to the next stage in worsted manufacture.

Drawing: During this process, the combed tops are gradually reduced from thick slivers of wool to what is usually described as roving from which the yarn is finally spun.

Spinning: The final stage in the conversion of wool to worsted yarn, the roving being drawn out to its final thickness and twist added for strength.

Twisting: Is the process in which two or more single spun yarns are united to produce a yarn of greater strength for use as warp threads in the weaving process and for normal knitting purposes.

Yarn Preparation: Reeling — spun yarns are formed into banks for dyeing or hand knitting yarns.

Winding — placing spun yarns onto packages suitable for the next process or for storage.

Balling — the more usual form of package for hand knitting purposes.

Warping: A large number of ends are wound, side by side, in a predetermined order, density and width, onto a beam for the loom.

Warp Preparation: Individual warp threads are drawn through a set of heald shafts according to pattern or twisted onto existing warp threads. Following drawing-in the threads are passed through the spaces in the reed. This controls the density and width of the cloth being woven.

Weaving: Where a loom is used to produce a piece of cloth by interlacing the warp threads — running the length of the fabric, with the weft threads — passing from side to side.

Perching: The woven fabric is inspected for faults and these are marked.

Burling & Mending: Any minor faults in the woven cloth are rectified by hand.

Dyeing: A wet process in which raw materials, yarns and fabrics have colour applied to increase their attractiveness.

Finishing: The fabric is treated by various processes to produce the required effect and handle.

# GLOSSARY

| | |
|---|---|
| Alley strap | Usually a piece of old leather belting fastened to a wooden handle. Used to waft fluff and dust under spinning frames to make the room look tidy. Overlookers sometimes chased and threatened workers with it. |
| Back-washing process | Cleaning process usually before combing to obtain the best colour of material in worsted manufacture. |
| B.D.A. | Bradford Dyers' Association. |
| Beef bah't bone | Snuff. |
| Bobbin | Reel onto which yarn or thread is wound on spinning frame. |
| Bobbin ligging | Putting empty bobbins onto the spinning frame. Usually the first job for a boy in the mill. |
| Box | French drawing machine which required a platform for the operative to stand on to reach the top of the machine. |
| Brayed | Hammered, struck with force. |
| Burling and mending | Correcting imperfections in cloth by pulling knots, slubs, etc. through to the back of the cloth. Mending broken threads, loose ends etc. |
| Cinderella Club | Local charity to help poor children, providing clothes, clogs, treats, holidays. |
| Continental shifts | 6 till 2. 2 till 10. 10 till 6. Brought in with new automatic machines which needed to be run continuously to recoup costs. |
| Divi | Dividend paid to co-operative members on goods purchased in Co-op stores. |
| Doffer | Young person of either sex but usually female, who removes full bobbins from spinning frames. |
| Flat cake | Bread made from left-over dough. |
| Jobber lad | Person who lubricates machines, fixes belts and generally assists the overlooker. Has usually progressed from being a bobbin ligger (so not necessarily a young lad). |
| Knocker-up | Person paid by workers to tap on bedroom windows with a long pole or stick to get them up for work. |
| Laking, laiking | 1. Playing about. 2. Not working, laid off. |
| Loom | Machine on which cloth is woven. |
| Loosed | Having finished an apprenticeship. |
| Minding | Looking after, being responsible for. |
| Noils | Shorter fibres combed from wool and discarded. Long fibres (tops) which are left are eventually spun into worsted yarn. |
| Overlooker | Usually male. Supervises workforce and keeps machinery running. |
| Penny hole, hoil, 'oil | Time keeping office next to mill gate. People coming late after mill gates were closed had money taken from their wages. |
| Piece | A length of fabric. Usually an accepted length between customer and supplier. |
| Piecener, Piecer, or 'picking ends up' | Person who joins or pieces together, by hand, threads broken during weaving or spinning. The resulting imperfections in the cloth would later be corrected by burling and mending. |
| Quartered | Loosing a quarter of a day's wages for being late. |

| | | | |
|---|---|---|---|
| Reeds | Several wires closely set between two slats separating the warp threads on a loom. | Tops | Long threads produced by combing wool. Used in spinning worsted yarn. |
| Roving | Thick yarn midway between a sliver and spun yarn. | Warp | Threads which run length-way in a piece of cloth. |
| Side minders | Pieceners | Weft | Threads that run cross-ways in a piece of cloth. |
| Skep | Large wicker basket used for storage of bobbins. | Willeying | Machine process of breaking open and disentangling fibres after washing and drying in preparation for carding. (Finer wools, eg. botany would be treated more carefully than coarse-bred wools and so would go through machines slower. |
| Taker off | Young person who takes off full bobbins from spinning frames and puts them into skeps. | | |
| Time-keeper | Person in the penny hole who noted latecomers' time of arrival. | | |

**All the quotations in this book have been taken from interviews with people involved in the Textile Industry in the Bradford area. All the interviews are anonymous at the request of the interviewees.**

**The following accession numbers indicate which interview each extract has been taken from, and are listed in the order in which they appear in the text.**

**Transcripts and sound recordings of the full interviews form part of the Oral History Collection in The Reference Library, 5th Floor, Central Library, Prince's Way, Bradford, BD1 1NN. Telephone Bradford 753688.**

**HOME & NEIGHBOURHOOD**

A0008; Anon; A0018; M0065; A0144; A0067; A0143; A0058; A0024; A0018; A0136.

**CHILDHOOD**

A0163; K0011; A0143; A0163; A0058; A0067; A0143; A0143; M0065; A0143.

**FIRST JOB**

A0026; A0161; A0163; A0114; FK0003; A0143; A0001; A0031; A0074; A0101; A0143; A0060; A0060; A0062; A0018; K0011; A0033; A0008.

**WOMEN IN THE MILL**

A0114; A0017; A0001; A0018; A0018; A0098; K0003; A0067; A0145; A0018; A0114; A0018; A0114; A0074; A0114; A0054; M0124; A0074; A0077; A0036; A0058; A0076.

**MEN IN THE MILL**

A0034; M0065; A0008; A0125; A0081; A0045; A0109; A0009; A0110; A0026; A0060; A0045; A0045; A0142; A0033.

**OTHER JOBS IN THE MILL**

A0060; A0110; A0055; A0009; A0062; A0012; A0062; A0045; A0070; A0144; A0062; A0125; A0034.

**WORK OUTSIDE THE MILL**

F002K; A0070; A0099; A0144; K0004; A0014; A0055; A0028; A0025.

**THE TRADE**

A0007; A0029; A0033; A0007; A0040; A0062; A0110; A0008; A0039; A0073; A0125; A0018; A0008; A0008; K0011; A0070.

**IMPORTED LABOUR**

B0103; A0033; A0018; B0046; A0144; Anon; A0036; A0110; B0071; B0016; C0016; Anon; A0043; C0123; A0008.

**SOCIAL LIFE**

A0143; A0036; A0145; A0018; A0020; A0156; A0145; A0023; A0045; A0110; A0143; A0164; A0168; A0055; A0058; A0009.